JAGUAR
D-TYPE

1954 onwards (all models)

Dedication

To Diane, for making a difference, and to JP and Will, as always.

First published in March 2017.

A catalogue record for this book is available from the British Library.

ISBN 978 1 78521 078 5

Library of Congress control no. 2016959354

Published by Haynes Publishing,
Sparkford, Yeovil,
Somerset BA22 7JJ, UK.
Tel: 01963 440635
Int. tel: +44 1963 440635
Website: www.haynes.com

Haynes North America Inc.,
859 Lawrence Drive, Newbury Park,
California 91320, USA.

Printed in Malaysia

Commissioning editor: Steve Rendle
Copy editor: Ian Heath
Proof reader: Dean Rockett
Indexer: Peter Nicholson
Page design: James Robertson

COVER IMAGE: Jaguar D-type
(Tony Matthews, 1986)

JAGUAR
D-TYPE

1954 onwards (all models)

Owners' Workshop Manual

An insight into the design, engineering, maintenance and operation of Jaguar's Le Mans-winning sports car

Chas Parker

Contents

7	Introduction

8	The D-type story

Dramatis Personae 10
The XK120 12
The XK120C or C-type 14
The D-type 17
1954 19
1955 21
1956 23
1957 26
1958 27
1959 onwards 29
D-type works drivers 29

40	Anatomy of the D-type

Chassis or front subframe 42
Front suspension 45
Central monocoque 48
Rear frame and suspension 52
Brakes 55
Steering 63
Bodywork 65
Engine 73
Transmission 81
Cockpit and instruments 85
Ancillaries 89
The finished article 94

98	The engineer's view

Chris Keith-Lucas – CKL Developments 100
Gary Pearson – Pearsons Engineering 104
John Pearson – Pearsons Engineering 105
Dick Crosthwaite – Crosthwaite and Gardiner ... 105

106	The driver's view

Ron Flockhart 108
Peter Sutcliffe 109
Chris Keith-Lucas 109
Paul Frère 109
Gary Pearson 110
John Pearson 110
Win Percy 110
Andy Wallace 114
Nick Faure 114
The passenger's view 116

118	The owner's view

Paul Michaels of Hexagon 120
Nigel Webb 120
Stefan Ziegler 123

124	Individual chassis histories

Works D-types 126
Other significant chassis 132

134	Restoration and historic racing

Restoration 136
Historic racing 145

146	D-type replicas

150	Appendix

D-type specification 150

154	Index

156	Bibliography

OPPOSITE The Ecurie Ecosse team scored a 1-2 at Le Mans in 1957, leading home a Jaguar D-type 1-2-3-4-6. Pictured is the second-placed car of Ninian Sanderson and Jock Lawrence (XKD 603). *(LAT)*

Introduction

'The D-type Jaguar, like the Spitfire, is a wonderful fusion of design, form and function. It was built to do a job, and when you do the sums to achieve that job, you end up with something that accidentally is extremely beautiful.'

The words are those of Chris Keith-Lucas, who's an acknowledged expert on Jaguars of all sorts and better placed than perhaps anyone else to speak with authority about one of the best-loved sports racing cars of all time. The D-type Jaguar was in production for a mere three years, between 1954 and 1957, yet it has become one of the most iconic models to have left the Browns Lane factory in Coventry, and one of the most famous and sought-after sports racing cars of all time. It was designed with one specific purpose in mind – to win the prestigious Le Mans 24-Hour race, a feat that it achieved on three consecutive occasions.

When I started writing this manual it was obvious that I needed to pull apart a D-type to examine it at close quarters. An opportunity to do this arose when chassis number XKD 570 – an original-specification car which was involved in an accident at the 2015 Le Mans support race – was sent to CKL Developments of Battle in East Sussex, only a 15-minute drive from my home, for a complete rebuild. Chris Keith-Lucas kindly gave me full access to the process, allowing me to take photographs at every stage of the procedure. In this way it has been possible to record a D-type Jaguar being assembled from the ground up.

Without the help of Chris and other members of his team at CKL, particularly MD Wicher (Vic) Kist, Mark Court, Olly Prosser, Tommy Coomber and John Smith, along with Nigel Baker at Kingswell Coachworks, also at Battle in East Sussex, this book would not have been possible. Acknowledgement must also be given to John and Gary Pearson of Pearsons Engineering in Roade, Northamptonshire, for their time and assistance with the project, particularly John who not only shared his extensive knowledge and archive on all things

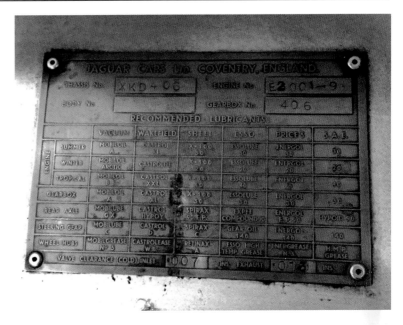

ABOVE The chassis plate for XKD 406, showing the chassis, engine and gearbox numbers, the recommended lubricants and valve clearances. *(Author)*

Jaguar, but whose patience, as I asked endless inane questions, knew no bounds. Thanks also to Dick Crosthwaite of Crosthwaite and Gardiner at Buxted, East Sussex, for his friendship and use of his extensive library.

Others who gave freely of their time and expertise were: Phil Cottrell, Nick Faure, Richard Heseltine, Paul Michaels, Win Percy, Phillip Porter, Paul Skilleter, Peter Sutcliffe, Andy Wallace, Nigel Webb and Stefan Ziegler. My thanks also go to Steve Rendle at Haynes for commissioning the project and for support and advice throughout, as always.

Finally, I am indebted in so many ways to my partner Diane, for her patience, encouragement and enthusiasm as I tried to write this alongside numerous other projects that were running in tandem. 'Thank you' is inadequate, but it will have to suffice for now.

Chas Parker
October 2016

OPPOSITE The author sits in D-type Jaguar XKD 543, which is owned by John Pearson and is the subject of the restoration project in chapter seven. *(John Pearson)*

Chapter One

The D-type story

Jaguar had long recognised that success in motor sport was a good way to promote road cars to the public at large. The company had already been victorious at Le Mans in 1951 and 1953 with its C-type model and enjoyed success in other events such as the Goodwood Nine-Hours and Reims 12-Hours, but now it wanted to take on the likes of Ferrari and Aston Martin and win convincingly in the high-profile French endurance event. The C-type, it was said, was made for competition, but the D-type was made to win.

OPPOSITE Privateers enjoyed considerable success racing D-types over many years. In 1961 Mike Salmon won the *Autosport* 3-Hours at Snetterton driving the ex-Ecurie Ecosse long-nose car, XKD 504. *(LAT)*

RIGHT Sir William Lyons, Jaguar managing director. *(LAT)*

BELOW Bill Heynes, chief engineer. *(LAT)*

BELOW RIGHT Lofty England, team manager. *(JDHT)*

ABOVE Malcolm Sayer, aerodynamicist. *(JDHT)*

RIGHT Phil Weaver, service department, then ran the competition shop. *(JDHT)*

BELOW Jack Emerson – engine development. *(John Pearson collection)*

BELOW RIGHT Norman Dewis – test and development driver. *(JDHT)*

With this in mind, all previous thinking was thrown out of the window and a completely original approach taken. The D-type was not an evolution of its predecessor the C-type, although it did share many components, including the straight-six XK engine, front and rear suspension and the use of disc brakes all round. Instead it drew heavily on aviation technology and aerodynamic know-how.

It was innovative. It consisted of a central cockpit section of monocoque construction, made up of riveted, double-skinned and box-section-supported aluminium alloy sheets. At the front an aluminium (subsequently steel) tube subframe, or chassis, carried the six-cylinder XK engine with its dry sump and gearbox, steering assembly and the wishbone and torsion bar front suspension. At the rear, a smaller subframe accommodated a Salisbury solid rear axle, mounted on trailing parallelogram links with torsion bars and telescopic damping. Fuel was carried in the tail inside a deformable Marston Aviation Division bag, rather than a conventional fuel tank.

The distinctive bodywork of the D-type was designed by Malcolm Sayer, an aerodynamicist who had joined Jaguar from the Bristol Aeroplane company. Sayer had also worked on the C-type and his aim was to reduce the frontal area of the car as much as possible and lower the centre of gravity. With this in mind, he produced a design of elliptical cross-section, with the engine canted over by 8°, resulting in the distinctive off-centre bulge in the bonnet. The under-body drag was reduced, increasing top speed, a tail fin was later added for extra aerodynamic stability, and in 1955 the works cars were fitted with a longer nose, increasing their length by 7½in.

The XK120

Despite it not being an evolution of its predecessors, the origins of the D-type can nevertheless be traced back to Jaguar's XK120 model. Launched at the 1948 London Motor Show, for which a single prototype was built, this revolutionary car, with its price tag of less than £1,300, stole the show. The name came from its twin overhead camshaft XK engine – designed by Bill Heynes, Claude Baily and Walter Hassan – which was one of the first of its type to be put into large-scale production, and its estimated top speed of 120mph.

The 120 was only ever intended as a limited production sports car, and because no full production run was envisaged the first cars were constructed from aluminium panelling over an ash and steel frame. Only

BELOW The Jaguar XK120 was launched at the 1948 London Motor Show. Standing behind it are Jaguar's main US distributors at the time, Max Hoffman (left, West Coast) and Charles Hornburg (East Coast). *(JDHT – Paul Skilleter collection)*

a small number of these were made before the car went into full production in May 1950, when pressed steel bodies were used. The majority of XK120s were exported to the USA and Australia, since supplies of scarce raw materials during this post-war period were only given to companies that exported a large percentage of their goods. Britain needed to earn foreign currency and the XK120, which could claim to be the fastest production sports car in the world, was highly desirable.

The XK120 made its competition debut on 20 August 1949 in the one-hour production saloon car race at the *Daily Express* International Trophy meeting at Silverstone, finishing 1–2 with drivers Leslie Johnson and Peter Walker at the wheel. It enjoyed further competition success in 1950, the cars again finishing 1–2 at Silverstone, this time with Peter Walker ahead of Tony Rolt, while Stirling Moss won the Tourist Trophy at Dundrod in Ulster in appalling conditions.

Three semi-works (privately entered but with help behind the scenes) XK120s were entered at Le Mans in 1950 for Leslie Johnson/Bert Hadley, Peter Clark/Nick Haines and Peter Whitehead/John Marshall. After 21 hours, Johnson's XK120 was lying third and running faster than the leading Talbot driven by Louis Rosier and his son Jean-Louis, but it retired

soon after with clutch problems. The other cars finished 12th and 15th respectively.

The XK120 rapidly became a favourite for amateurs and professionals alike. At the production sports car race for cars over 3,000cc at the 1951 Silverstone International Trophy meeting, no fewer than ten XK120s started the race and every one of them finished. The event was won by Stirling Moss ahead of Charles Dodson, and XK120s filled the top five positions.

ABOVE Leslie Johnson and Peter Walker finished 1-2 at the 1949 *Daily Express* International Trophy meeting at Silverstone on the car's competition debut. (LAT)

BELOW Five XK120s lined up at the start of the production saloon car race at the 1951 International Trophy at Silverstone: 35 is Charles Dodson, who would finish second, 34 George Wicken (fourth), 32 Bill Holt (eighth), 31 G.N. Gee (12th) and 30 Duncan Hamilton/Philip Fotheringham-Parker (third). The race was won by Stirling Moss in another XK120. (LAT)

The car was also being raced across the world in the USA, Cuba, Italy, Finland, Switzerland, Portugal, Argentina and France, as well as at numerous club events in the UK, while Ian Appleyard and his wife Pat (daughter of Jaguar founder Sir William Lyons) were victorious in the Alpine Rally from 1950–52 in their XK120 registration number NUB 120, demonstrating the car's ability to succeed in all types of competition.

The XK120C or C-type

The road-going XK120 was eventually followed in 1954 by the XK140, and then in 1957 by the XK150 (top speed 150mph), but by then Jaguar had already developed a new competition car specifically aimed at Le Mans. It was felt that if a dedicated racing version of the already successful XK120 could be built, then the goal of winning Le Mans could be achieved. The result was the XK120C (the 'C' standing for competition), which eventually became known just as the C-type. It was launched in 1950 and used the XK120's six-cylinder XK engine, which had been modified to produce around 200bhp. The car featured a tubular chassis, independent front suspension with a trailing link at the rear and was developed by Bill Heynes. The body shape, as already mentioned, was designed by Malcolm Sayer, and the C-type was built

at the Swallow Road works at Foleshill, prior to Jaguar's move to Browns Lane in Coventry. Its construction was overseen by Phil Weaver, superintendent of the competition department.

Three works cars were entered at Le Mans for 1951, to be driven by Peter Walker/Peter Whitehead, Stirling Moss/Jack Fairman and Leslie Johnson/Clemente Biondetti; the cars were given a send-off at the factory before being driven down to Le Mans for the race by team manager 'Lofty' England, Jack Emerson and Phil Weaver. Moss was the early leader in the race, and after four hours – and with the second-placed Talbot Lago driven by Froilán González and Onofre Marimón in the pits to refuel – the Jaguars held the first three places. Half an hour later, though, the Johnson/ Biondetti car retired with low oil pressure. The other two C-types remained at the head of the field chased by the Talbot-Lagos of González/ Marimón and Louis Rosier/Juan Manuel Fangio until, soon after midnight, Moss' car suffered the same oil pressure problem as its sister and was out, leaving just the Walker/Whitehead C-type to uphold Jaguar honours. This it did in style, taking Jaguar's first victory at the famous circuit ahead of the Talbot-Lago of Pierre Meyrat and Guy Mairesse.

The second outing for the C-type was the Tourist Trophy at Dundrod in Northern Ireland, in which Stirling Moss led a 1-2-4, followed by two

BELOW The team of C-type Jaguars for the 1951 Le Mans 24-Hours lined up outside the Browns Lane factory. The winning car (number 20 – XKC 003) of Peter Walker and Peter Whitehead sits alongside that of Leslie Johnson/ Clemente Biondetti (number 23 – XKC 001) and Stirling Moss/Jack Fairman (number 22 – XKC 002). *(LAT)*

victories at Goodwood's September meeting. It was also during 1951 that Jaguar began to develop disc brakes in collaboration with Dunlop.

The following year a single C-type, driven by Stirling Moss and Norman Dewis, was entered for the punishing Mille Miglia event. It ran well before retiring with a broken steering rack mounting. Le Mans, however, turned out to be a disaster for the company. Jaguar entered three lightweight, streamlined, long-nose C-types with elongated tails for Stirling Moss/Peter Walker, Tony Rolt/Duncan Hamilton and Peter Whitehead/Ian Stewart. The aerodynamic changes unfortunately resulted in overheating problems, and within four hours all three Jaguars had retired.

However, matters were put right in 1953. Jaguar went away, licked its wounds and returned with a heavily revised C-type design, including thinner-gauge aluminium body, rubber-bag fuel tanks, increased engine power via three triple-choke Weber carburettors, and its now fully developed disc brakes. The company entered three cars for Le Mans, driven by Stirling Moss/Peter Walker, Tony Rolt/Duncan Hamilton and Peter Whitehead/Ian Stewart.

Despite factory opposition from Ferrari, Cunningham, Aston Martin, Alfa Romeo, Talbot-Lago, Lancia and Gordini, the race boiled down to a battle of green versus red, as Jaguar and Ferrari fought to take victory. Stirling Moss was the early leader, chased by the Ferraris of Luigi Villoresi/Alberto Ascari with teammates Rolt and Hamilton in third. Moss encountered fuel problems that dropped him down the field, leaving Rolt/Hamilton to battle

it out with Villoresi/Ascari at a frenetic pace for the remainder of the race. Eventually the pace proved too much for the Ferrari, which began to slip back with clutch problems, while Moss and Walker slowly worked their way back up to second. At the flag, Rolt and Hamilton took victory with teammates Stirling Moss and Peter Walker in second place. The third works C-type of Whitehead and Stewart was fourth, behind the Cunningham of Phil Walters and John Fitch.

ABOVE The winning C-type Jaguar of Peter Walker and Peter Whitehead at the 1951 Le Mans 24-Hours. *(LAT)*

BELOW Jaguar finished 1-2 at Le Mans in 1953, Tony Rolt and Duncan Hamilton leading home teammates Stirling Moss and Peter Walker. The third C-type of Peter Whitehead and Ian Stewart finished fourth. *(LAT)*

RIGHT On 20 October 1953 the 'light alloy car', driven by Norman Dewis and fitted with a Perspex 'bubble' over the cockpit, recorded an average speed of 178.383mph (287.018kph) over the flying mile at Jabbeke in Belgium. *(Paul Skilleter collection)*

THE LIGHT ALLOY CAR

Nestled between production of the C-type and the D-type, as a sort of interim stage, was the so-called 'light alloy car', though it was also known at different times as the XK120C Series II (or Mark II), the C/D Prototype or D-type Prototype, the XKC 054 and the XKC 201. This prototype, which was made in 1953, was a clear evolutionary step between the C-type and the eventual D-type. It was designed by Malcolm Sayer and featured a semi-monocoque chassis with a magnesium tube frame welded by the argon arc process and an elliptical opening at the front replacing the traditional grille, a feature which would carry through to a number of subsequent Jaguars.

The car was fitted with engine number E1002-8 and included a Salisbury rear axle, rack-and-pinion steering and disc brakes. It was first tested at Lindley on 13 May 1953 by Jaguar's regular test driver, Norman Dewis, and again on 17 May, when a half-shaft broke. On 20 October it was fitted with a Perspex 'bubble' over the cockpit and taken to Jabbeke in Belgium for high-speed runs, where it averaged 178.383mph (287.018kph) over the flying mile, but the engine seemed to suffer from fuel starvation and would not pull cleanly at the top end.

One of the modifications subsequently made was the introduction of a head fairing to replace the 'bubble', something that would become a distinctive feature of the D-type. With an all-synchromesh gearbox and SU carburettors replacing the Webers, the car was tested again at Silverstone by Dewis in November and later by Tony Rolt. It was reported to go through corners well and the steering was said to feel good, although the rear end bounced and produced wheelspin at full power. Despite this, Dewis concluded that the car was 'very stable and controllable'.

During December Dewis tried out a new type of Dunlop tyre, while in January 1954 Stirling Moss tested the car, complaining of too much understeer and suggesting that the pedal layout and position of the steering wheel required modifying. Gradually, the final specification for the D-type was being drawn up.

BELOW Test driver Norman Dewis stands alongside the light alloy car at Jabbeke. *(John Pearson collection)*

The D-type

In the meantime, Jaguar's rivals, such as Ferrari, weren't standing still either but were fast developing new cars. Jaguar was not content, or confident, in merely developing its C-type model. It became clear that in order to maintain its hard-won domination at Le Mans Jaguar required a revolutionary new car – lighter, stiffer and more aerodynamic. But after its crushing success in 1953, why was it so important to continue winning at Le Mans?

'There was this huge level of interest at the time in Le Mans, and it really was a vehicle through which car sales could be achieved,' explained Chris Keith-Lucas of CKL Developments. 'There was much greater interest in it then than there is now, sadly, even though it remains a big thing to this day. And quite clearly, Jaguars just wouldn't stand still at the time.

'I think that we forget the amazing rate of change during the 1950s and early '60s. We're seeing that sort of change now only in electronics, but at the time it was in engineering, and people were moving forward at an amazing rate. The Apollo moon landings and Concorde are prime examples, but in terms of cars, if you look at something like a Ford GT40, which though it still looks like an incredibly modern design came only ten years after the D-type, that was the speed at which things were developing.

'So already by 1954 they thought that the spaceframe was old hat and that monocoque design was the way things were going, and possibly this was to reflect what was happening with their production cars. The production cars, they knew, were going to go monocoque, and they wanted their cutting-edge race car perhaps to be a monocoque too. I don't know if that was the thinking, but it might have been part of it. And by doing that they were able to achieve a weight saving, and a very big frontal-area saving by going to the elliptical cross-section instead of a basically rectangular cross-section, such as the C-type. They were able to knock the corners off, decrease the frontal area and achieve a much greater top speed. So there were a whole lot of reasons.'

On 8 February 1954 Jaguar issued a long document, summarised here, detailing the intended specification for the new car, which at that time was still unnamed.

Engine

Cylinder head	Standard XK type with inlet valve increased to 1⅞in, exhaust valve to 1⅝in, not using salt-cooled valves.
Pistons	Brico 9:1, latest design.
Camshaft	Wide angle timing, ⅜in lift.
Carburettors	Three Weber 45 DCO with special packing under the intake pipe to allow for the engine to be set over at 8½°.
Cylinder block	Change to front bearing cap to permit dry sump lubrication to be fitted and modified drilling on the rear face to suit smaller clutch housing.
Lubrication	Dry sump lubrication. (It was noted that this would be one of the most difficult items to get clear and tested in time.)
Oil radiator and oil tank	This had yet to be finalised.
Clutch	Triple-plate clutch with special flywheel ring to suit new starter position. Strength of springs and counterweights to be discussed with Borg & Beck. It was also noted that it was important to ensure that an adequate supply of these clutches would be available for their requirements.
Engine mountings	It was proposed to have main engine mountings at the front and rear of the gearbox, with lower-rated mountings adjacent to the rear face of the cylinder block.
Alternative engine specification	35/40 head with 9:1 compression ratio and normal valves or, alternatively, with 10:1 compression ratio and salt-cooled valves. This head could also incorporate ⁷⁄₁₆in lift camshafts. Engine and various parts had been despatched to Weslakes to carry out tests.
Petrol injection	Both SU and Lucas had devised petrol injection systems for the Jaguar engine, the SU system having already been tested and shown good results.

Body and chassis

The body was designed by Malcolm Sayer and construction was to be as for the light alloy car, with the outside skins being produced by Abbey Panels. Argon arc welding was to be used. At this time items such as attachment of the rear body to the frame, method of support for front outriggers, mounting of radiator, air duct and airbox for the carburettors, bonnet louvres and cooling for the rear brakes had yet to be decided.

Petrol tanks

These were to be made of plastic by ICI. It was suggested that a second, smaller, tank holding three to four gallons be located behind the rear diaphragm in the tail.

ABOVE **Jaguar chief engineer Bill Heynes sits in the prototype D-type with unpainted aluminium bodywork. Note the brick supporting the exhaust pipe!**
(Philip Porter collection)

Front suspension

Same as on the light alloy car but with new top arms with a greater spread and bottom arms re-splined at a slight angle to enable the torsion bar to be moved away from the driver's ankle.

Rear suspension

This was to be basically the same as used towards the end of the 1953 racing season on the C-types, with torque arms top and bottom at either end of the axle and a Panhard link for control.

Hubs

New hubs would be required as it was proposed to abandon wire wheels and change to knock-on aluminium wheels.

Brakes

The brakes were to be basically as used the previous season but probably with a Dunlop instead of a Girling master cylinder, dependent on results of tests. Brake pedals were to be of the pendant type and hinged well forward. Handbrake position and method of operation were still to be decided.

Clutch operation

At the time it was planned to use hydraulic operation, although direct-rod operation would be preferable as it permitted quick adjustment for wear.

Gearbox

The only gearbox available was the standard one as used the previous year. However, Jaguar was working on a four-speed box that would give an additional usable ratio and possibly enable an overdrive top, leaving the two lower ratios basically the same. An alternative Borg & Beck overdrive was also being considered.

Propshaft

Hardy Spicer type. Investigations were under way on a shaft modified by Metalastik to give a degree of flexibility, but no practical tests had been carried out.

The very first D-types, built in 1954, had an aluminium alloy frame, or chassis, for which Jaguar, in collaboration with the British Oxygen Company, pioneered the technique of argon arc welding. Subsequent models, from 1955 onwards, used a removable steel chassis in order to make repairs easier.

One major difference between the D-type and the light alloy car was the use of a dry-sump lubrication system, which allowed the engine to be lowered and the frontal area of the car reduced. The dry sump system was developed by Jaguar's chief engineer William Heynes along with Walter Hassan, a former Bentley engineer. The engine was tilted over at $8\frac{1}{2}°$ from vertical, to provide extra space for the carburettor assembly, necessitating an offset bulge in the bonnet. Phil Weaver drew on his experience in the aircraft industry when it came to the design of the dry sump tank, which was based on that of the Hercules aero engine fitted to the Beaufighter. The tank had to be triangular in shape in order to fit within the frame but the internal baffling was just as in the Beaufighter.

1954

Early models followed the existing XKC chassis numbering system since, at that time, Jaguar hadn't planned to call the new model the 'D-type'. Six cars were built – XKC 401 to 405 (though 405 was subsequently broken up and used for spare parts to repair damaged cars) and XKD 406, the factory now recognising the official name of D-type for the new car.

On 13 April 1954, XKC 401 was tested at Lindley by Norman Dewis, who reported that the engine was misfiring. The following day he tried it again, still experiencing the misfire, but also noting that the car jumped out of second gear, the steering was 'dicey', the seating uncomfortable and the pedal layout poor. In addition, the clutch was heavy to operate and the brake pedal hard to 'feel'. Gradually, the problems were ironed out and a further three D-types were constructed.

1954 competition history

The D-type made its racing debut at the 1954 Le Mans 24-Hours, the cars being driven down to the circuit as was common practice for Jaguar in those days. Three 3.4-litre cars were entered by the works team: XKC 403 (registration number OKV 2) for Stirling Moss and Peter Walker, XKC 402 (OKV 1) for Tony Rolt and Duncan Hamilton and XKC 404 (OKV 3) for Peter Whitehead and Ken Wharton. However, all three suffered from problems with the fuel filters. After these were removed the car driven by Hamilton and Rolt ran well and eventually finished less than a lap behind the winning Ferrari. It achieved 172.8mph on the Mulsanne Straight, against the 4.9-litre Ferrari's top speed of 160.1mph. The other two D-types failed to finish.

There was more success at the Reims 12-Hours in July, with Whitehead/Wharton in

BELOW Duncan Hamilton and Tony Rolt finished second on the D-type's racing debut at the 1954 Le Mans 24-Hours in XKC 402. *(LAT)*

ABOVE The 1957 Jaguar XKSS. *(LAT)*

BELOW On 12 February 1957 fire swept through the Jaguar factory at Browns Lane, destroying nine cars and damaging many others. *(JDHT)*

PRODUCTION D-TYPES AND THE XKSS

Apart from the cars supplied to the Ecurie Ecosse team, which were effectively 'production' cars, the first private owner of a D-type was Duncan Hamilton, who acquired XKC 402 (registered OKV 1) in early 1955, which he campaigned during the subsequent three seasons. Other private owners included Jack Broadhead (XKD 403 – OKV2). Hamilton also acquired XKD 406, which was driven on a number of occasions by drivers such as Michael Head and Peter Blond.

A proper manufacturing line for the D-type didn't start until mid-1955, when assembly began at the Browns Lane plant, with delivery of the first car in August that year. The cost of a new D-type was £3,878, including Purchase Tax. It was intended that the production run would be 100 cars but this was later reduced to 67. The first true production car was XKD 509, which was exported new to California. Eventually only 42 were sold and delivered, with 18 going to the USA, ten staying in Britain, three going to Australia, two to France and one each to Belgium, Canada, Cuba, East Africa, Finland, Mexico, New Zealand, El Salvador and Spain.

With the end of competition in 1957 there was a problem with surplus production D-types left unsold. On 21 January 1957 it was announced that the remaining 25 D-types would be converted into road-going versions, named the XKSS, for export only at a quoted price of $6,900.

The car was described by *The Motor* in its 30 January 1957 edition: 'Developed from the successful D-type racing sports car, a new two-seater Jaguar has made its appearance in response to demand from America for a car combining racing performance with equipment and weather protection of touring-car standard. The new Jaguar, to be called the XK "SS" should meet this demand in a most potent and satisfying manner, for it follows the mechanical specification of the 3½-litre Le Mans cars in all essentials, yet has a full-width curved windscreen, folding hood, luggage grid and bumpers. The cockpit is properly trimmed, has well-upholstered seats and a full "touring" range of instruments. Features retained from the D-type include the large tail fuel tank, drilled lightweight steering wheel, and Dunlop disc brakes and light-alloy disc wheels with knock-off hubs. The car is initially for export only, and first deliveries will be made in February to the USA, where the price is $6,900. The XK "SS" is an addition to the Jaguar range and will not supplant any existing model.'

However, on the evening of 12 February 1957 a fire broke out at Browns Lane, gutting the factory and destroying nine of the 25 cars being built there. All equipment and tooling was also destroyed.

Over its lifetime, total D-type production consisted of 18 factory cars, 53 customer cars and 16 XKSS versions.

XKC 404 leading home Rolt/Hamilton in XKC 402 for a 1-2 victory. Again, Moss and Walker failed to finish. The best the D-types could manage at the Tourist Trophy at Goodwood in September, though, was sixth for Whitehead/ Wharton in XKC 403 and 14th for Moss/Walker in XKD 406, with Rolt/Hamilton in XKC 402 being the ones to record a DNF this time.

1955

For the following year a number of modifications were made to the design of the D-type. The front subframe, or chassis, was now constructed of steel tubing rather than aluminium, and bolted to the monocoque rather than welded, the old method being difficult to repair. The new frame was extended through the monocoque to the rear bulkhead.

A separate frame carried the radiator and oil cooler and was attached by bolts. For the works cars the cylinder head was redesigned to give more power, with 2in inlet valves and exhaust valves $1^{11}/_{16}$ in diameter. The inclination of the exhaust valves on the works cars was changed from 35° to 40° to stop them fouling the larger inlet valves, and with these wide-angle 35/40 heads, as they were known, output was now around 270bhp. The most noticeable modification was the adoption of a long nose by the works cars, for better aerodynamic penetration.

The chassis numbering of the 1955 cars onwards continued to reflect the fact that they were now officially known as 'D-types', being designated XKD 5-- (the '5' denoting that they were constructed in 1955). The first two cars, XKD 501 and 502, went to the Scottish Ecurie Ecosse team, while Ecurie Francorchamps had XKD 503. XKD 504–508 were the five long-nose works cars and differed in other details as well, having two brake cooling ducts in the bonnet, the third headlamp that had been fitted to the nearside of the 1954 cars removed, the two remaining headlamps uprated to 100W and the exhaust pipes routed to the rear of the car instead of the side.

The D-types were raced extensively during 1955, not just by the works team but also by private individuals and teams such as the Edinburgh-based Ecurie Ecosse outfit and Briggs Cunningham in the US. The Cunningham team won the Sebring 12-Hours, with Mike Hawthorn/Phil Walters driving XKD 406, while Duncan Hamilton, in XKC 402 which he had bought in January that year, took third place at the Dakar 2 Hours and the Goodwood Easter Monday meeting, and then went on to finish runner-up at the Coupes de Paris.

The works team came in third, fourth and fifth at the *Daily Express* International Trophy meeting at Silverstone in May behind the Aston Martin DB3Ss of Reg Parnell and Roy Salvadori, before heading for Le Mans the following

ABOVE **Peter Whitehead and Ken Wharton won the 1954 Reims 12-Hour race in XKC 404.** *(LAT)*

ABOVE Mike
Hawthorn and Ivor
Bueb gave the D-type
its first Le Mans
victory in 1955, the
occasion marred by
the accident that
claimed the lives of
over 80 spectators
along with that of
Mercedes driver Pierre
Levegh, leading to the
withdrawal of the rest
of the Mercedes team.
(LAT)

month. Three cars were entered here – Mike
Hawthorn and Ivor Bueb in XKD 505 (trade
plate 774 RW), Tony Rolt and Duncan Hamilton
in XKD 506 (732 RW) and Don Beauman and
Norman Dewis in XKD 508 (194 WK). For the
first time the cars were transported by air rather
than driven down to the circuit.

The race developed into a fierce duel
between the Hawthorn/Bueb D-type and the
Mercedes SLR of Juan Manuel Fangio and
Stirling Moss. The two cars traded the lead,
lapping everyone up to sixth place, until three
and a half hours into the race when an accident
in front of the pits, involving the Mercedes of
Pierre Levegh and the Austin-Healey of Lance
Macklin, claimed the lives of over 80 spectators.
Levegh also perished in the accident, which is
thought to have been triggered by Hawthorn
slowing to come into the pits. Hours later the
Mercedes team withdrew, leaving Hawthorn to
take a somewhat subdued victory. The Ecurie
Francorchamps D-type, driven by Johnnie Claes
and Jacques Swaters, came in third.

Like their predecessors, D-types were also
enjoying considerable success in private hands,
though these were standard, short-nose varieties.
Duncan Hamilton campaigned his own D-type, as
did other top sports car drivers of the day such
as Michael Head and Bob Berry. Later names

such as Mike Salmon, Peter Blond and Ian Baillie
also campaigned D-types with success.

There was a single works entry for Mike
Hawthorn (XKD 506) at the British Grand Prix
meeting in July but he could only manage fifth.
The next victory for a D-type came courtesy of
Ecurie Ecosse, with Desmond Titterington (XKD
501) finishing first at Charterhall in August 1955
and then again at Snetterton the following week,
where he led an Ecurie Ecosse 1-2 ahead of
teammate Ninian Sanderson (XKD 502). The
pair also finished runners-up in the Goodwood
Nine-Hours that month, driving XKD 501. Further
success for the Ecosse team followed at Crimond
and Aintree, while Duncan Hamilton took wins
at Silverstone and Snetterton and privateer Alex
McMillan had a hat-trick of victories at Silverstone
in October driving XKD 517.

Overseas, Sherwood Johnston drove Briggs
Cunningham's XKD 507 to victory at Watkins
Glen, Hagerstown and Nassau that year, and
Jack Rutherford won at the Nassau Speed Trials
in XKD 516. Two weeks into 1956 Johnston
and Jerry Austin won the Six Hours Torrey Pines
event in Austin's XKD 527, while the following
month Charles Brown took XKD 527 to victory at
Mansfield. Johnston continued his run of victories
in March, this time driving Briggs Cunningham's
car at the SCCA National at Walterboro.

1956

Revised regulations for 1956, known as 'Appendix C', meant that the cars had to be modified in order to comply. A full-width, 25cm-high windscreen was required, as was the provision of a passenger door and adequate leg room on the passenger side – a passenger entering the car from the driver's side had to climb across to the passenger seat, which on a D-type wasn't possible due to the central strip through the cockpit. The solid tonneau cover on the passenger side was no longer allowed, so Malcolm Sayer came up with a Vybak clear plastic tonneau, which ran from the top of the screen to the back of the passenger seat in order to minimise aerodynamic drag. In addition the capacity of the fuel tank had to be decreased from 36.5 gallons (166 litres) to 28.6 gallons (130 litres).

During 1954 the 'light alloy car' had been fitted with both Lucas and SU fuel injection systems. Tests showed that the Lucas PI (Petrol Injection) system gave 25% better fuel consumption and a 'general overall improvement in performance characteristics'. In late 1955 Jaguar's Experimental Department carried out further tests with more encouraging results and so the first of the 1956 cars to be built, XKD 601, was fitted with the Lucas PI system.

The works team built six long-nose cars for the 1956 season, but for their first outing of the year – the Sebring 12-Hours in March – took two 1955 cars (XKD 506 for Bill Spear/Sherwood Johnston and 508 for Duncan Hamilton/Ivor Bueb) and only one of the new batch, XKD 601, for Mike Hawthorn/Desmond Titterington, running with the Lucas fuel injection system. All three retired, while Alfonso Gómez-Mena and Santiago González brought XKD 521 home in eighth and the Briggs Cunningham XKD 507, driven by Cunningham and John Gordon Bennett, came in 12th.

Ron Flockhart gave Ecurie Ecosse its first victory of the season at Snetterton in March, driving XKD 561, and then followed this up with victory at the Goodwood Easter meeting. Walt Hansgen scored a win in XKD 529 at the SCCA Regional at Thompson in the USA and Duncan Hamilton took his own car to victory at the Prix de Paris in April. The Charterhall meeting that month gave the Ecosse team further success, with Flockhart winning a *Formule Libre* event in XKD 502 and Sanderson the unlimited sports car race in the same car.

The next outing for the works team was the *Daily Express* International Trophy at Silverstone in May, which turned into something of a disaster. Three cars were entered – Hawthorn in XKD 603 with fuel injection, Titterington in XKD 604 (with de Dion rear suspension – the only time this was tried on a D-type – and carburettors) and Fairman in XKD 504 with carburettors. None of the three finished. Titterington spun on the first lap, triggering a multi-car pile-up, while Fairman retired with a broken driveshaft. Hawthorn challenged at the front but retired with a seized ball joint, although not before setting fastest lap. Bob Berry, driving Jack Broadhead's XKC 403, had more luck, coming home third, while the Ecurie Ecosse trio of Alan Brown (XKD 502), Ron Flockhart (XKD 561) and Ninian Sanderson (XKD 501) recorded fourth, sixth and DNF respectively.

In the US, Harold Fenner won at Mansfield in May in XKD 541 while Curt Lincoln took XKD 530 to victory at Eläintarhanajo in Finland.

More wins came for Alex Millan (XKD 517) at Silverstone and Ninian Sanderson (XKD 502) at Spa. In the US, at Bakersfield, Bill Krause scored a victory in Clem Atwaters' XKD 519, and there were wins for Walt Hansgen (XKD 529) at Cumberland and Eagle Mountain, for Ernie Erickson in XKD 503 at Lawrenceville, and Jack Ensley (XKD 538) at Smartt Field in Missouri. Desmond Titterington took a win at Goodwood for Ecurie Ecosse in XKD 502 and

---

D-TYPE VARIANTS

- 1954 aluminium frame, short-nosed. Construction differed to all subsequent models.
- 1955 and 1956 customer or production cars, steel frame.
- 1955 five works long-nosed, steel-frame cars (never sold to customers).
- 1956 long-nosed works cars.
- Unsold production cars then converted to XKSS specification.

ABOVE Ecurie Ecosse driver Ron Flockhart had to retire XKD 501 from the 1957 Mille Miglia when rough roads, combined with a heavy fuel load, caused the tail of the car, which contained the fuel tank, to break away from the monocoque. The wire fence that Flockhart went through can be seen wrapped around the rear of the car while the Vybak cover over the passenger seat appears to have remained intact. *(John Pearson collection)*

BELOW Ecurie Ecosse took a famous 1-2 at Le Mans in 1957, with Ron Flockhart/Ivor Bueb leading home teammates Ninian Sanderson/Jock Lawrence in their D-types. *(LAT)*

LEFT Jimmy Stewart won the Johnson's Sports Car Challenge Trophy at the Goodwood Whitsun meeting on 7 June 1954 in his Ecurie Ecosse C-type Jaguar, ahead of teammate Ninian Sanderson. *(LAT)*

ECURIE ECOSSE

It was always stressed that there was no official connection between the Edinburgh-based Ecurie Ecosse team and the works, and that Ecosse was just a customer that happened to be given first refusal to purchase the previous year's team cars from the factory at very competitive prices.

Ecurie Ecosse was established by accountant David Murray and 'Wilkie' Wilkinson and was based at Merchiston Mews, Edinburgh. Murray owned and raced a Maserati that Wilkinson prepared, along with the Jaguar XK120s of Ian Stewart and Bill Dobson. Deciding to pool resources and aim to earn prize money as a team, they brought Sir James Scott-Douglas on board and, with a little backing from Esso, the Ecurie Ecosse team was formally announced in January 1952. Their first outing was at Charterhall on 6 April that year when Dobson won an unlimited scratch race ahead of Stewart.

During 1953 the team ran four C-type Jaguars, a Cooper-Bristol and a Connaught. Dobson retired but Ninian Sanderson and Jimmy Stewart joined, the team competing in both club events and major sports car races. In 1954 they won a number of events using the ex-works C-types from the previous season. For 1955 they acquired ex-works D-types, but it was in the following year that they enjoyed their greatest success to date, entering Le Mans for the first time with a single car for Ron Flockhart and Ninian Sanderson. After the works cars dropped out, the Ecosse entry was left to battle with the Aston Martin of Stirling Moss and Peter Collins, eventually taking victory by a single lap.

This success was surpassed the following year when the team's two cars, driven by Ron Flockhart and Ivor Bueb, and Ninian Sanderson and Jock Lawrence, finished 1-2 at Le Mans. Although continuing to compete for many years thereafter, the team never achieved quite this level of success again.

Bob Berry scored a victory at the same meeting in XKC 403.

The works team headed for the Nürburgring 1,000km next, with Hawthorn/Titterington in XKD 601 and Paul Frère/Duncan Hamilton in XKD 603. Frère crashed 603 badly during practice, and Norman Dewis had to drive out a replacement, XKD 504, from the UK. He managed the 700-mile journey just in time for Frère to start the race, albeit from the back of the grid as the car had missed practice. Alas, the efforts proved in vain as the gearbox eventually broke and the car was retired. Hawthorn and Titterington retired with a broken half-shaft on the last lap.

There was more success in June at the Reims 12-Hours, when Bueb/Hamilton (XKD 605) led Hawthorn/Frère (XKD 601) and Titterington/Fairman (XKD 603) to a 1-2-3 victory.

Le Mans was to prove another outstanding success for the D-type, although it was the blue of Ecurie Ecosse that took the honours rather than the green of the works team. The works took three cars along for Mike Hawthorn/Ivor Bueb (XKD 605), Paul Frère/Duncan Hamilton (XKD 606, which was crashed in practice and replaced by XKD 603), and Jack Fairman/Ken Wharton (XKD 602). In addition to these, Ecurie Ecosse and Equipe Nationale Belge each sent a single car for Ron Flockhart/Ninian Sanderson (XKD 501) and Jacques Swaters/Freddy Rouselle (XKD 573) respectively.

Hawthorn was comfortably quickest in practice and led away at the start, chased by the Aston Martin DB3S of Stirling Moss. On the second lap, Frère was caught out by the wet track and spun XKD 603 in the Esses, hitting the barrier. Fairman, who was following in XKD 602, spun himself in avoidance and

was collected by the Ferrari of the Marquis de Portago, all three cars having to retire from the race. Soon afterwards, Hawthorn brought the sole surviving works car, XKD 605, into the pits with a misfire (eventually traced to a cracked fuel line), dropping right back down the field.

This left the Ecurie Ecosse car of Flockhart and Sanderson to battle it out with Moss, co-driving with Peter Collins, in the Aston, the pair taking turns to lead the race. Gradually the Jaguar began to ease away and eventually took the chequered flag ahead of the Moss/Collins Aston and Olivier Gendebien/Maurice Trintignant's Ferrari. The Equipe Nationale Belge D-type came in fourth, while Hawthorn and Bueb had made their way back up to sixth at the finish. Ecurie Ecosse had won Le Mans at their first attempt.

Back home, Peter Blond won at Snetterton in XKD 518 and Jock Lawrence was victorious in Ecurie Ecosse's XKD 561 at the Goodwood Trophy second handicap event. Henry Taylor won in XKD 517 at Silverstone and Bob Berry in XKC 403 at Oulton Park.

Wins kept coming in the States as well, Walter Huggler taking XKD 523 to victory at Allentown, and Loyal Katskee in XKD 536 at Stillwater, while Walt Hansgen won at the SCCA National at Thompson International Speedway and again at the one-hour event there in September. The same month, George Constantine drove XKD 545 to victory at Watkins Glen and Bill Browning won at Chester in a D-type, chassis number unknown. John Fitch took a brace of wins in the Briggs Cunningham-entered D-type at Thompson Speedway in October, as did Hansgen at the same track three weeks later. Bill Krause won at Willow Springs in XKD 519 while John Fitch,

ABOVE The winning Ecurie Ecosse D-type, driven by Ron Flockhart and Ninian Sanderson, at the 1956 Le Mans 24-Hours. *(LAT)*

in Cunningham's XKD 507, won at Nassau in December. At the same meeting, Marion Lowe gave the D-type its last victory of the year in the second ladies' heat driving XKD 509.

At the end of the season the works Jaguar team withdrew from competition and sold XKDs 504, 603 and 606 to the Ecurie Ecosse team.

1957

It didn't take long for a D-type to notch up its first victory of 1957, Bob Gibbons winning at Ardmore in New Zealand in XKD 534. In the States, Jerry Austin won at Paramount Ranch in March in XKD 527, Jack Ensley at Boca Raton in XKD 538 and Lou Brero at Stockton in XKD 509. Pete Woods won twice in Hawaii in XKD 528 and Walt Hansgen in XKD 605 at Lime Rock in April. There were two more victories for Bill Krause at Willow Springs in XKD 519.

At May's Goodwood meeting, both Ian Baillie and Maurice Charles took wins in XKD 511 and 502 respectively, while Julio Mariscal won in XKD 554 at Puebla and Lago de Guadalupe in Mexico. John Fitch took another win for Briggs Cunningham at Thompson Speedway and

Ron Flockhart won the 2 Hours of Forez in the ex-works XKD 603 for Ecurie Ecosse, ahead of Jock Lawrence in XKD 504 and Duncan Hamilton in his privately owned XKD 601. The wins in private hands continued thick and fast as well. William Klinck in XKD 524 took two victories at Dunkirk in the USA, while Jack Ensley won twice at Harewood Acres in Canada and Pete Woods in XKD 528 at Paramount Ranch.

Five D-types were entered for Le Mans in 1957, and all five finished. Ecurie Ecosse had two cars for Ron Flockhart/Ivor Bueb (XKD 606) and Ninian Sanderson/Jock Lawrence (XKD 603). Duncan Hamilton entered XKD 601 for himself and Masten Gregory while Paul Frère and Freddy Rouselle drove the Equipe Nationale Belge entry (XKD 573). The final entry, XKD 513, was driven by Jean Lucas and 'Mary', the pseudonym used by Jean-Marie Brussin.

A furious battle evolved, initially between the works Ferraris, Maseratis and Aston Martins, but the pace was to prove too much, leaving Flockhart and Bueb to lead home a D-type Jaguar 1-2-3-4-6 ahead of teammates Sanderson and Lawrence. Lucas and Brussin were third, Frère and Rouselle fourth and

BELOW Ron Flockhart and Ivor Bueb, driving the Ecurie Ecosse-entered XKD 606, led home a Jaguar 1-2-3-4-6 at the 1957 Le Mans 24-Hours. *(LAT)*

Hamilton/Gregory in sixth behind the Ferrari of Stuart Lewis-Evans and Martino Severi. It doesn't get much better than that.

Immediately after Le Mans, the Ecosse cars were taken to Monza to participate in the 'Race of Two Worlds', or 'Monzanapolis' as it was dubbed, a 500-mile event conceived by the United States Automobile Club (USAC) and the Automobile Club di Milano for Indianapolis cars to go head-to-head against Formula One machinery using Monza's banking to create an oval course. However, the event was boycotted by the Formula One teams and the only non-Indianapolis entries were the three D-types from Ecurie Ecosse for Jack Fairman (XKD 603), Jock Lawrence (XKD 606) and Ninian Sanderson (XKD 504). The race was run in three heats, and Fairman managed to snatch the lead at the start of the first heat and led at the end of the first lap, but the D-types were outpaced by their American opposition. They were, however, more reliable, and as the Indy cars fell by the wayside during the three races the Jaguars kept circulating, to finish a highly respectable fourth, fifth and sixth on aggregate.

Also in the States, C.K. Thompson won at Courtland and Walt Hansgen twice at Marlboro Raceway in XKD 529 and once at Montgomery in XKD 508, and then again in Briggs Cunningham's car at Thompson Raceway, Watkins Glen and Bridgehampton. Henry Taylor drove the Murkett Brothers' XKD 517 to victory at Snetterton.

Don Skogmo won in XKD 536 at Milwaukee and Bill Krause twice in XKD 519 at Willow Springs. George Constantine took XKD 545 to victory at Thompson while Wallace/Hansgen won in the Cunningham car at Virginia.

1958

The rules were changed for the 1958 Le Mans with engine size limited to 3.0 litres. Jaguar developed a 3.0 engine but it was unreliable and uncompetitive compared to the competition. While the works engine was built by reducing the size of the 3.4-litre block, Ecurie Ecosse's 'Wilkie' Wilkinson experimented with increasing the bore and stroke of the 2.4-litre engine. Without proper development, none of the 3.0-litre variants could be described as a success.

ABOVE Jack Fairman takes XKD 603 high on the Monza banking during the 1957 'Race of Two Worlds' at which the cars ran anticlockwise around the track. Fairman led at the end of the first lap but finished fourth overall on aggregate. *(LAT)*

The 1958 season didn't start well for Ecurie Ecosse. The team entered the Sebring 12-Hours for the first time with Ron Flockhart/Masten Gregory in XKD 603 and Ninian Sanderson/Ivor Bueb in XKD 504, but both dropped out before the halfway mark with valve problems in the new 3-litre version of the XK engine. At the Nürburgring 1,000km event three cars were entered and the new engines proved more reliable, though the best result the team could manage was Fairman/Lawrence in XKD 606 in ninth place. Bueb/Sanderson (XKD 504) retired with front suspension damage while Gregory/Flockhart (XKD 603) spun off and crashed.

At Le Mans, where the team was aiming for a hat-trick of wins, just two cars were entered – XKD 603 for Fairman/Gregory, and XKD 504 for Sanderson/Lawrence. It was to prove a disaster, however, as both cars retired within the first half-hour with broken pistons. It was later surmised that the problems had been caused by the fuel supplied at the circuit causing detonation problems, leading to piston failure, but this was never proved.

Other D-types were also unsuccessful. Maurice Charles in XKD 502 was injured when he crashed in heavy rain, while Jean-Marie Brussin, who was sharing XKD 513 with André Guelfi, crashed during the night and was killed. Duncan Hamilton in XKD 601, partnered by Ivor Bueb, was running well but crashed trying to avoid a backmarker.

Ecurie Ecosse licked its wounds and returned to Monza for the second, and last, running of the 'Race of Two Worlds', with D-types for Masten Gregory and Ivor Bueb and a Lister for Jack Fairman. The D-types finished last of the runners in all three heats. Gregory and Bueb were 15th and 16th respectively in heat one and Bueb 11th in heat two, Gregory deciding not to continue. Bueb was seventh, but still last, in the third and final heat.

In the four-hour Tourist Trophy at Goodwood, the team entered XKD 504 for Gregory and Innes Ireland, the pair finishing in fifth place, with Duncan Hamilton and Peter Blond sixth in Hamilton's own car.

Private entrants of D-types, particularly in the USA, continued to race their cars successfully. Among their victories in 1958, in chronological order, were:

- Walt Hansgen – Cunningham car, Miami
- Jim Rattenbury – XKD 558, Abbotsford
- Jim Clark – Border Reivers XKD 517, Full Sutton (two wins)
- Jimmy de Villiers – XKD 512, Grand Central
- Jim Clark – Border Reivers XKD 517, Full Sutton (two wins)
- Harry Carter – XKD 529 – Thompson
- Jim Clark – Border Reivers XKD 517, Full Sutton (two wins)
- Jim Clark – Border Reivers XKD 517, Mallory Park

BELOW Ivor Bueb in XKD 603, was the only D-type driver to complete all three heats of the 1958 'Race of Two Worlds', albeit finishing last in all three. Note the huge air scoop to feed cold air to the tyres.
(LAT)

- Jim Rattenbury – XKD 558, Deer Park
- Walt Hansgen – Cunningham car, Bridgehampton (two wins)
- Jimmy de Villiers – XKD 512, Angola
- Ron Flockhart – Ecurie Ecosse XKD 606, Charterhall
- Blackwell/Miles – XKD 528, Pomona 6-Hours

1959 onwards

By 1959 the D-type was being outclassed in international sports car racing, and Ecurie Ecosse ran a single example (XKD 603) at Le Mans for Ireland and Gregory. The car ran as high as second place at one point, until its works-supplied short-stroke engine blew up. Wins abroad that year included:

- Mauricio Miranda – XKD 549, San Salvador
- Jean-Guy Pilon – car unknown, St Eugene (four wins)
- Bruce Boyle – XKD 523, Vineland
- Joe Grimaldi – XKD 523, Vineland
- Ed Rahal – XKD 553, Daytona

And so it went on. The D-type continued to be the car to beat in club racing with drivers such as Peter Sutcliffe, John Coundley, Maurice Charles, Gerry Ashmore, Peter Sargent, David Wansbrough, James Boothby, Peter Skidmore, Peter Blond and Mike Salmon at the wheel. Salmon won the *Autosport* 3-Hours at Snetterton in 1961 driving an ex-works and ex-Ecurie Ecosse D-type, XKD 504.

But by the early '60s the D-type had become far less competitive against newer, lightweight and rear-engined machinery such as the Cooper T49 and Lotus 19. It was to undergo a comeback, however, with the advent of an historic racing series for cars of its type. Using the same car (XKD 504) in which Mike Salmon had won the *Autosport* 3-Hours five years previously, Neil Corner won the first ever Griffiths Formula meeting at Castle Combe in 1966. The series went on to become the birthplace of the Historic Sports Car Club, and the D-type has been run at numerous historic meetings ever since, with drivers such as Willie Green, Martin Morris, 'Willie Eckerslyke' (pseudonym for Nigel Moores) and Anthony Bamford at the wheel.

D-type works drivers

Don Beauman

Don Beauman was born on 26 July 1928 and took up racing a Cooper 500 in 1950 and then in 1953 a Riley TT Sprite, lent to him by his friend Mike Hawthorn. He won at Goodwood, Ibsley and Thruxton and also took part in the Nürburgring 1,000km sharing a Frazer Nash Le Mans Replica with its owner Michael Currie, the pair finishing 11th.

In 1954 he drove a Connaught A-type, owned by Sir Jeremy Boles, and won *Formule Libre* races at Oulton Park and Brands Hatch. He also drove an Aston Martin DB3, also owned by Boles, and scored a class win at Zandvoort, finishing fifth overall. Beauman took part in just one Formula One Grand Prix, the 1954 British event at Silverstone driving the Connaught, where he finished 11th. Later that year he finished fourth in the Oulton Park Gold Cup, third at Snetterton and second in the Madgwick Cup at Goodwood.

In 1955 he shared a works D-type Jaguar (XKD 508) at Le Mans with Norman Dewis, the pair retiring after getting stuck in the sand bank at Arnage. On 9 July that year Beauman was competing in the Leinster Trophy at Wicklow in Ireland when he crashed his Connaught after having just set the fastest lap in the handicap event. The car hit a tree and caught fire, killing Beauman instantly.

Ivor Bueb

A garage owner from Cheltenham, Ivor Bueb was born on 6 June 1923 and started racing in 500cc events in 1952. His success led to a works drive with Cooper in 500cc Formula Three for 1955. He finished second to teammate Jim Russell in the British Championship and shared the winning Jaguar D-type at Le Mans that year with Mike Hawthorn.

He continued to run in Formula Three

throughout 1956, but also won the Reims 12-Hours for Jaguar with Duncan Hamilton and scored his second Le Mans 24-Hour victory driving an Ecurie Ecosse D-type partnered with Ron Flockhart.

Bueb made his Formula One debut at the 1957 Monaco Grand Prix driving a works Connaught, and in 1958 he drove for Bernie Ecclestone's Connaught team at Silverstone and in a Lotus-Climax 12 at the Nürburgring, retiring in each. Bueb was also running a private Lotus-Climax 12 in Formula Two events and driving for Lister in sports car races, scoring a number of victories for the team during 1958–59.

In 1959 he also raced in the British Saloon Car Championship for Equipe Endeavour driving a 3.4-litre Jaguar, taking three wins from three starts. That year he joined BRP (British Racing Partnership, managed by Alfred Moss and Ken Gregory) but was killed when he crashed the team's Formula Two Cooper-Borgward T51 in the Trophée d'Auvergne at Clermont-Ferrand and was flung from the car, dying in hospital six days later on 1 August 1959.

Norman Dewis

Norman Dewis was Jaguar's chief test and development driver from 1952 to 1985, helping to develop cars such as the C-type, D-type, XK140 and 150, 2.4 and 3.4-litre Mk2 saloons, MkVII, E-type, XJ13, XKS and XJ40.

Born on 3 August 1920, Dewis worked for Armstrong Siddeley before the Second World War and then joined the RAF as a rear gunner. At the end of the war he joined Lea Francis testing new cars but in 1951 he was head-hunted by Bill Heynes at Jaguar. Dewis took charge of the company's test programme, initially trying out the Dunlop disc brakes on a C-type. In 1952 he was selected as co-driver to Stirling Moss on the Mille Miglia, but the pair retired with broken steering.

On 20 October 1953, during a series of speed tests on the motorway at Jabbeke in Belgium, Dewis achieved a speed of 174.412mph in a streamlined XK120, a record for a production car.

Dewis was instrumental in the development of the D-type and particularly its Lucas petrol injection system. In 1955 he co-drove with Don Beauman in a factory D-type at Le Mans, the pair having to retire when lying fourth after Beauman crashed. Later in the year, partnered with Bob Berry, he finished fifth in a privately entered D-type at the Goodwood Nine-Hours.

In 1971 he was testing the experimental XJ13 at the MIRA test track when a tyre deflated and he crashed heavily, the car rolling, thankfully without injuring him. Dewis estimates that he covered over one million test miles for Jaguar, finally retiring aged 65 in 1985. He was awarded an OBE in the 2015 New Year's Honours list.

Jack Fairman

John (Jack) Fairman was born on 15 March 1913 in Smallfield, near Horley in Surrey. His first competitive outings were in trials and hill climb events and he also raced at Brooklands pre-war before serving in the Royal Tank Regiment. In 1949 he finished eighth at Le Mans, sharing an HRG-Singer with Eric Thompson, the pair winning their class. In the 1951 event he drove for Jaguar, sharing a C-type with Stirling Moss and leading before retiring with engine failure.

With a background in engineering, Fairman became an accomplished test and development driver. He helped develop the Connaught Formula Two and the Type-A Formula One cars, the latter leading to a drive in the 1953 Italian GP, though he had already made his Grand Prix debut at Silverstone that year in an HWM.

He drove a Type-B Connaught in the British and Italian Grands Prix in 1956, finishing fourth and fifth respectively. He also drove in the 1957 and 1958 British Grands Prix – for BRM in the former and Connaught (by now owned by Bernie Ecclestone) again in the latter, retiring from both events. He finished eighth in a Cooper T45 at the 1958 Moroccan Grand Prix and raced for Cooper again in the British and Italian events in 1959 and the British in 1960, but again not making the finish in any of them.

It was in sports cars that Fairman made his name, racing for Bristol, Jaguar, Ecurie Ecosse and Aston Martin, where he won twice in 1959 as co-driver to Stirling Moss. Later that year, at Goodwood, Moss took over the second-placed DBR1 that Fairman was sharing with Carroll Shelby and took it to victory, securing the World Championship for Aston Martin. Fairman died on 7 February 2002.

Paul Frère

Born on 30 January 1917, Paul Frère started racing motorbikes in 1946, but switched to cars and shared an MG PB with Jacques Swaters in the 1948 Spa 24-Hours. In 1952 he won a production sports car race at the same circuit. Also that year he joined the HWM Formula Two team at the GP des Frontières at Chimay, narrowly beating the Connaught of Ken Downing to victory. This win led to him making his Formula One debut that year for HWM at

the Belgian Grand Prix, where he finished fifth at a very wet Spa.

Frère demonstrated his wet weather skill once again at the 1953 Eifelrennen at the Nürburgring, where he finished second, and also scored class wins that year in the Mille Miglia and at Le Mans. In 1955 he finished second at Le Mans in a works Aston Martin DB3S shared with Peter Collins.

A fourth place in his home Grand Prix at Spa Francorchamps in 1955, driving a Ferrari 555 Supersqualo, led to Frère replacing the injured Luigi Musso at Ferrari the following year at the Belgian Grand Prix. Driving one of the Lancia-Ferrari D50s, he finished second behind teammate Peter Collins.

It was in sports cars that he really made his name, finishing second in the 1956 Reims 12 Hours, driving a Jaguar with Mike Hawthorn, before winning the event in both 1957 and 1958 with fellow Belgian Olivier Gendebien for Ferrari. His greatest triumph, however, was victory in the 1960 Le Mans 24 Hours, again with Gendebien, in a Ferrari 250TR.

At the end of 1960 Frère retired from racing to pursue his other career as an automotive journalist, becoming European editor for the American publication *Road & Track* magazine, and was the author of many books. He died on 23 February 2008.

BELOW
Duncan Hamilton.
(LAT)

Duncan Hamilton

Born on 30 April 1920, Hamilton attended the Aeronautical Engineering College at Chelsea and Brooklands before joining the Fleet Air Arm in the Second World War. After the war he opened a garage and started competing in sprints and hillclimbs using an MG R-Type, soon to be replaced by a Bugatti. In 1948 he purchased a Maserati 6CM and raced this at Zandvoort and Goodwood. For 1949 he went into partnership with Philip Fotheringham-Parker to run the Maserati in as many events as possible, his best placing being second in the *Formule Libre* handicap at Goodwood in September.

The following year he won the Easter handicap at the same circuit and shared a 3.4-litre Nash-Healy with Tony Rolt at Le Mans, the pair finishing fourth. Later in the year Hamilton won the 3-litre class of the production saloon car event at the International Trophy meeting at Silverstone in a Healey Silverstone. Further success came with victory in the 100-mile handicap Wakefield Trophy at the Curragh circuit in Eire driving his Maserati and later the second September handicap at Goodwood.

In 1951 he acquired a Jaguar XK120 and finished third in the over 2-litre production sports car race at the Silverstone International Trophy. At the same meeting he drove a Talbot-Lago T26C in the main event and, in torrential rain, passed the Alfa Romeos of Juan Manuel Fangio, Felice Bonetto and Consalvo Sanesi. He eventually finished second behind the 'Thin Wall Special' Ferrari of Reg Parnell when the race was abandoned after six laps due to the conditions.

Hamilton competed in the British, Dutch and German Grands Prix driving the Talbot-Lago and continued to race his XK120, scoring a brace of victories at Boreham and a pair of second places at Goodwood. 1952 was mainly spent driving a Formula Two HWM-Alta in European Grands Prix, as well as competing in his own C-type, the first to be sold to a private owner. He drove for the works Jaguar team at Le Mans but all three works C-types retired early.

The following year was more successful, with Hamilton sharing the winning C-type at Le Mans with Tony Rolt. Soon after, he crashed heavily at Oporto in Portugal driving his own C-type and suffered serious injuries, although he was

back racing later in the year at Goodwood and Dundrod but without success.

Hamilton acquired his own D-type Jaguar in 1954 and took this to victories at Goodwood, Silverstone and Snetterton. Le Mans brought retirement, however, in the works D-type. The following year, paired with Ivor Bueb, he took victory for the team at the Reims 12-Hours but was immediately sacked by Jaguar for disobeying team orders and not letting teammate Paul Frère win.

Hamilton continued to campaign his own D-type throughout 1957–58 but retired from racing at the end of the 1958 season to concentrate on his garage business and to pursue his new interest of yachting. He died on 13 May 1994.

Mike Hawthorn

Known by the French as *Le Papillon* ('The Butterfly') due to his habit of wearing a bow tie while racing, and as the 'Farnham Flyer' by his British fans, Mike Hawthorn was the first British driver to win the Formula One World Championship, though his name was also forever linked with the tragic accident at the 1955 Le Mans which claimed the lives of over 80 spectators.

It was perhaps no surprise that Hawthorn would become a racing driver, since his father Leslie owned the Tourist Trophy garage in Farnham, Surrey, and raced motorcycles himself. Born on 10 April 1929, Hawthorn junior first competed at the 1950 Brighton Speed Trials in a Riley Ulster Imp, winning the 1,100cc sports car class. That year he won a number of events including the Ulster Trophy handicap at Dundrod and the Leinster Trophy at Wicklow.

He won his first single-seater race in a Cooper-Bristol at Goodwood in 1952 and made his Formula One debut at the Belgian Grand Prix that year, finishing fourth. He also took third at the British Grand Prix at Silverstone. For 1953 he drove in Formula One for Ferrari, winning the French Grand Prix at Reims that year and finishing fourth overall in the drivers' championship. He also won the International Trophy at Silverstone and the Ulster Trophy, while in sports cars he won the Spa 24-Hours in a Ferrari, partnered by Giuseppe Farina.

The following year he suffered serious burns after crashing at Syracuse but took victory at the Spanish Grand Prix later in the year. When his father died in a road accident he inherited the family business, so for 1955 he left Ferrari to join Vanwall in order to be closer to home. However, this lasted for just two races and he returned to Ferrari for the rest of the season.

That year he had also joined Jaguar as a works driver and, together with Ivor Bueb, took victory in a D-type (XKD 505) at Le Mans. The race was marred by the accident that occurred when Hawthorn braked sharply to stop at the pits, causing the following Healey of Lance Macklin to swerve into the path of Pierre Levegh's Mercedes, which was launched into the crowd. Hawthorn was cleared in an official inquiry but his name was forever linked with the tragedy, and the somewhat hollow victory that followed after the Mercedes team withdrew its remaining cars. The following year he and Bueb finished sixth in the event.

In Formula One, a change to BRM for 1956 was unsuccessful and the following year he rejoined Ferrari, a second place at the Nürburgring being his best result. 1958 was to be his championship year, despite only winning one Grand Prix, the French at Reims, against the four of Stirling Moss, but he took second-place finishes in Belgium, Britain, Portugal, Italy and Morocco. At the end of the season he announced his retirement from racing.

On 22 January the following year Hawthorn was driving his 3.4-litre Jaguar Mk1 on the A3 Guildford bypass when he crashed into a tree and was killed instantly.

ABOVE

Mike Hawthorn (right).
(LAT)

Stirling Moss

Often hailed as the greatest driver never to win the World Championship, Stirling Moss was born on 17 September 1929 and started racing in 1948 aged just 18, in a Cooper-JAP 500, scoring his first victory on 4 July that year at Brough Aerodrome. He won his first major international race on the eve of his 21st birthday at the wheel of a Jaguar XK120 in the 1950 RAC Tourist Trophy at Dundrod.

Moss drove for Jaguar at Le Mans on four occasions, three times in a C-type (1951–53) and once in a D-type (1954). Success was to elude him at this track though, and his best finish for Jaguar was in 1953 when he and Peter Walker came home second. He also finished runner-up in the 1956 event, driving an Aston Martin DB3S with Peter Collins. On every other occasion he failed to finish the race. Moss also competed in a number of rallies, finishing second in the 1952 Monte Carlo in a Sunbeam-Talbot.

In 1954 he campaigned his own Maserati

250F in Grands Prix, which led to a works Mercedes drive the following year to partner Juan Manuel Fangio. His first Grand Prix victory came at the 1955 British Grand Prix at Aintree in a Mercedes W196, and the same year he triumphed in the Mille Miglia in a Mercedes 300 SLR, partnered by Denis Jenkinson, as well as the Targa Florio and the Tourist Trophy at Dundrod.

He was back in the Maserati 250F for 1956, winning at Monaco and Monza, and drove for Vanwall during 1957, winning the British Grand Prix at Aintree after taking over Tony Brooks' car, and again at Pescara and Monza.

Other outstanding drives of his career included winning the 1958 Argentine Grand Prix in a Cooper-Climax T43 – the first such success for a rear-engined Formula One car – and the 1961 Monaco Grand Prix in Rob Walker's Lotus 18, beating the more powerful Ferraris.

Moss finished runner-up in the Formula One World Championship four times in succession, from 1955–58, and third in each of the following three years. He took part in 66 Grands Prix, winning 16 and taking 16 pole positions, driving for Mercedes-Benz, Maserati, Vanwall, Rob Walker, Cooper and Lotus.

At the start of the 1962 season, Moss crashed his Lotus heavily at Goodwood on 23 April and was in a coma for a month. Although he recovered, he decided that his reactions were slower than they had been and decided to retire from racing. His exploits are too numerous to mention individually. In total he competed in 527 races, finished 375, winning 212 of them. He was knighted in the 2000 New Year's Honours List.

Tony Rolt

Tony Rolt was born on 16 October 1918 and educated at Eton before joining the Royal Military Academy at Sandhurst. He acquired a Triumph Southern Cross when he was 17 and entered the 1936 Spa Francorchamps 24-Hour race, finishing fourth in class with his friend Jack Elliot as co-driver. He bought ERA 'Remus' from Prince Bira and, aged just 19, was victorious in the British Empire Trophy at Donington driving it in 1939.

At the outbreak of war he joined the army and became an officer in the Rifle Brigade. In May 1940 he was captured and taken prisoner of war at Dunkirk. Later, having escaped from seven prisoner-of-war camps, he was sent to the high-security Colditz Castle in July 1943, where he was part of the escape committee that tried to build a glider to escape from the castle. The camp was liberated in 1945 before the glider ever flew.

When the war was over he soon resumed racing, campaigning an Alfa Romeo, a Delage and a Nash-Healy. He shared Peter Walker's ERA at the 1950 British Grand Prix at Silverstone. The same year he had his first race in a Jaguar, an XK120 belonging to Nick Haines, and came second to Peter Walker at Silverstone. In 1951 he raced Rob Walker's Delage, and took second place – albeit in an HWM – at the 1952 International Trophy behind his teammate Lance Macklin.

Rolt continued to race for Walker in 1952–53 in a Connaught, winning a number of Formula Two, *Formule Libre* and handicap races. Paired with Duncan Hamilton he drove for the works Jaguar team, winning Le Mans in 1953 and finishing runner-up the following year. The pair also came in second at that year's Reims 12 Hours.

Rolt retired from racing in 1955 to concentrate on his family business and died on 6 February 2008.

Desmond Titterington

Desmond Titterington was born in Northern Ireland on 1 May 1928. He took up racing an MG in 1950 and the following year finished second at Phoenix Park in Dublin in a Fiat Balilla. During 1952–53 he raced an Allard J2, winning the 1952 Wicklow Trophy.

In 1954 Titterington joined Ecurie Ecosse, racing the team's C-type Jaguar in national events. He won at Oulton Park and was sixth at the British Grand Prix sports car race. He also took victories in a Triumph TR2 at Goodwood and Kirkistown.

For 1955 Titterington was racing one of Ecurie Ecosse's new D-type Jaguars, winning the Ulster Trophy and taking further victories at Charterhall and Snetterton. This led to a works drive and he shared a D-type with Mike

Hawthorn in the Tourist Trophy, the pair retiring. The same year he was offered a drive with Mercedes and shared a 300SL with John Fitch in the Targa Florio, finishing fourth.

Deciding to try his hand at Formula One, Titterington drove a Vanwall at the Oulton Park Gold Cup in September 1955 and came third

ABOVE
Tony Rolt. *(LAT))*

BELOW
Desmond Titterington.
(JDHT)

behind Stirling Moss and Mike Hawthorn. He continued with the Connaught in 1956, came third in the BRDC Trophy at Aintree and second at the International Trophy at Silverstone. His only championship outing was at the 1956 British Grand Prix, from which he retired.

Titterington continued to race Jaguars for both the works and Ecosse teams in 1956, winning at Goodwood for Ecosse and finishing third in the Reims 12-Hours for the works team with Jack Fairman. At Le Mans he was entered in a works D-type with Paul Frère but the Belgian crashed out early in the race.

At the end of the year Titterington retired to concentrate on his business. He died on 13 April 2002.

Peter Walker

Born on 7 October 1912, Peter Walker's greatest claims to fame were winning the 1951 Le Mans and the 1953 Goodwood Nine-Hours. Serious injuries from a crash in 1956 curtailed his career.

Known as 'Skid' Walker because of his aggressive driving style, he began racing Peter Whitehead's ERA in 1935, taking wins at Brooklands and Donington Park. He took part in

the 1948 RAC British Grand Prix at Silverstone, again in an ERA, and finished 11th. The same year he set FTD at the Prescott Hill Climb and came second at one of the opening events at Goodwood.

A works drive for Jaguar resulted in a second-place finish at the International Trophy at Silverstone in 1949 at the wheel of an XK120. The following year he won the event. In 1950 he shared an ERA E-type with Tony Rolt at the British Grand Prix, the pair retiring. In May 1951 he tested the new Jaguar XK120C, or C-type, beating the time set by Stirling Moss. This was the prelude to his victory at Le Mans in the car that year, partnered by Peter Whitehead.

Despite suffering severe burns a month later driving a BRM V12 at the British Grand Prix, Walker drove a C-type in the Tourist Trophy at Dundrod, finishing second behind Moss in a Jaguar 1-2-3. He and Moss retired from the 1952 Le Mans but the pair charged through the field the following year after initial delays to finish second. 1954 brought little success and he left Jaguar to join Aston Martin for 1955. Victory in the Goodwood Nine-Hours, teamed with Dennis Poore in a DB3S, was his sole victory that year.

A bad crash in a DB3S at the 1956 Le Mans curtailed his driving activities. He died on 1 March 1984.

Ken Wharton

Born on 21 March 1916, Ken Wharton first competed at Donington Park at the wheel of an Austin, aged just 19. He became a motor engineer with his own Ford dealership in Birmingham and built his own 'specials', taking part in trials and hillclimbs, and competed in 500cc Formula Three events in a Cooper-JAP, taking a win at Zandvoort.

It was in hillclimbs and rallies that he really excelled, travelling through Europe in 1951 with an ERA and winning the British Hill Climb Championship every year from 1951 to 1954. He also won the Tulip Rally in 1949 in a Ford Anglia, again in 1950 driving a Ford Pilot, and finally in 1952, this time at the wheel of a Ford Consul.

In 1952–53 he competed regularly in national events at the wheel of a Frazer Nash Le Mans Replica, winning at Boreham and Snetterton and taking top-three places at Thruxton and Goodwood. He also finished second in the 1953 British Empire Trophy at Douglas on the Isle of Man.

Wharton took part in 15 World Championship Grands Prix, making his debut in Switzerland at the wheel of his Frazer Nash in 1952 and finishing fourth. He retired in Belgium and Holland that year but came ninth at the wheel of a Cooper T20 in Italy. He raced a Cooper T23 in 1953, his best results being seventh in Switzerland and eighth in the British event at Silverstone. For 1954 he raced a Maserati 250F entered by the Owen Racing Organisation and also drove the V16 BRM, winning the Glover Trophy at Goodwood. In 1955 he joined Vanwall but crashed in the Silverstone International Trophy and suffered burns to his arms and neck.

In sports cars Wharton drove for the works Jaguar team in 1954, winning the Reims 12-Hours at the wheel of a D-type shared with Peter Whitehead. He and Whitehead also drove for the factory at Le Mans that year but retired. Later in the year they finished sixth at the Tourist Trophy at Dundrod.

In 1955 he drove his own Aston Martin DB3S in a handful of events while 1956 saw him at the wheel of a number of cars including an Alfa Romeo 6C 3000 belonging to Jo Bonnier, which he took to tenth place in the British Empire Trophy, a Maserati 330S, a Ferrari 750 Monza and a 290MM. He had a single outing for Jaguar in a D-type at Le Mans, partnered by Jack Fairman, but the pair retired.

At the end of 1956 Wharton finished third in the Australian Tourist Trophy in Melbourne driving a Ferrari 750 Monza but on 12 January 1957 he was killed when he crashed the same car in a sports car race at Ardmore in New Zealand.

Peter Whitehead

Peter Whitehead was born on 12 November 1914 and started racing a Riley when he was 19, before buying an ERA that he shared with Peter Walker in the Donington Grand Prix of 1936, the pair finishing in third place. In 1938 he took the ERA with him on a prolonged business trip to Australia and won the Australian Grand Prix at Bathurst, together with the Australian

Hill Climb Championship, before returning to England in 1939.

Whitehead flew with the RAF during the Second World War but took up racing again in 1947, taking his ERA to second place in the British Empire Trophy on the Isle of Man. He purchased a Ferrari 125 in 1949, becoming the first person to whom Enzo Ferrari ever sold a Formula One car, but only scored a single podium finish in 11 Grands Prix between 1950 and 1954.

He shared a Jaguar XK120 with John Marshall at Le Mans in 1950, finishing 15th, but came second at that year's Tourist Trophy. In 1951 he and Peter Walker took the first victory for Jaguar at Le Mans driving a C-type. This led to a works Jaguar drive at Le Mans in 1952 at the wheel of a C-type with Ian Stewart, the pair retiring. The following year, again in a C-type, Whitehead and Stewart finished fourth. His final outing at the circuit as a works driver was in 1954, partnered with Ken Wharton in one of the new D-types, but they retired with gearbox failure after completing 131 laps.

He and Wharton were more successful that year in the Reims 12-Hours, winning the event

LE MANS

In the 1950s one race mattered more than any other – the Le Mans 24-Hours. It was the jewel in the crown of sports car racing, and immense international prestige was attached to winning the event. Le Mans was the most important sports car race in the world – the severest test to which a production model could be put. It received wide-ranging coverage in the press, and was far better known to the general public in those days than it is today.

The event was conceived as a way of allowing the French motor industry to demonstrate the safety, reliability, convenience and economy of the motor car as a mode of everyday transport in the years following the First World War. Only production cars were eligible to enter, and it was not intended to be a race but rather a demonstration of reliability, with each car set a minimum distance that it was required to complete during the 24 hours, according to its engine capacity. The 'winner' would be the car that exceeded its target distance by the greatest amount. However, no winner would be declared, since the competition was triennial and intended to be run over three consecutive years, in the first case 1923–25. Those cars that exceeded their target distance qualified for the following year's event, where the same thing would happen, and the overall winner wouldn't be established until the third running, when the winner would receive the Rudge-Whitworth Cup. In the meantime, the next running would have started in the second year, the winner of that event being declared another two years later, and so on.

It is not surprising that this complicated affair was overshadowed in the minds of the press and the public by whoever had covered the greatest mileage in the 24-hour period – in other words, the winner of each separate event.

The first *Vingt-Quatre Heures du Mans*, or *Grand Prix d'Endurance* as it was known, was held on 26–27 May 1923, the winner – that is the car exceeding its target distance by the greatest amount –

in their D-type. It was Whitehead's second consecutive win there, having partnered Stirling Moss to victory in a C-type the previous year. As well as his Jaguar commitments, Whitehead also campaigned a Cooper T33 in 1954, victory at Snetterton being a highlight.

1955 brought little success. He raced a Cooper T38 and shared Duncan Hamilton's D-type Jaguar with Michael Head at the Goodwood Nine Hours, the pair retiring. He had more success, though, racing in the southern hemisphere during 1956–57. Driving his Ferrari 125, he took victory in the Lady Wigram Trophy in New Zealand in 1954 and repeated the feat in 1956 and 1957 in a Ferrari 500 and 555 respectively. He also won the Rand Grand Prix and finished in the top three in a number of other events.

Throughout 1957 he drove an Aston Martin DB3S and the following year he and his half-brother Graham shared the driving in it at the Nürburgring 1,000km, where they finished eighth, and at Le Mans, taking the runners-up spot in June. Three months later, on 12 September 1958, they were competing in the Tour de France when their 3.4-litre Jaguar Mk1 crashed into a ravine, killing Peter instantly. Graham survived but with serious injuries.

being the Salmson AL of Lucien Desvaux and Georges Casse. However, what we would call the 'winner' – the car that covered the greatest distance during the 24 hours – was the Chenard-Walker of André Lagache and René Léonard. Two years later it was Chenard-Walker that won the first (and only) Triennial Cup, the award being replaced in 1924 by a Biennial Cup. From 1928 a conventional 'winner' was recognised in the form of the Annual Distance Cup, going to the car that had covered the greatest distance.

In 1924 the car that achieved this had a been a 3-litre Bentley – the only non-French car entered – driven by Captain John Duff and Frank Clement. It was to be the start of a long line of successes for the British company, for although La Lorraine was to triumph in 1925 and 1926, Bentley then took the honours in 1927–30, establishing the legend of the 'Bentley Boys' and putting Le Mans firmly in the minds of car manufacturers and motoring enthusiasts alike. To win at Le Mans was seen as the pinnacle of motor sport achievement. Alfa Romeo then took over the reins, winning the event from 1931–34. The following year's race was cancelled but it was French cars – first Bugatti, then Delahaye and then Bugatti again – which triumphed in 1937–39.

Ferrari won the first post-Second World War race in 1949, while a French Talbot-Lago was victorious the following year. In 1951 Jaguar scored its first Le Mans victory when the XK120C of Peter Walker and Peter Whitehead took the honours, followed by further victories in 1953 (Tony Rolt and Duncan Hamilton in a C-type), 1955 (Mike Hawthorn and Ivor Bueb in a works D-type), 1956 (Ron Flockhart and Ninian Sanderson in an Ecurie Ecosse-entered D-type) and 1957 (Ron Flockhart and Ivor Bueb in another Ecurie Ecosse D-type). That year D-type Jaguars filled five of the top six places, finishing 1-2-3-4-6. It was the car's greatest triumph.

BELOW The start of the very first Le Mans 24-Hours, held in 1923. (LAT)

Chapter Two

Anatomy of the D-type

There are approximately 3,000 rivets in a D-type, the main structure of which can essentially be broken down into three components – the front subframe, or chassis, the central monocoque and the rear frame. While the C-type was built around a tubular frame, with main members taking the loads and body panels only playing a small part in its structural integrity, the D-type was built around an elliptically shaped central section monocoque which provided extra strength, rigidity and weight reduction.

OPPOSITE XKC 401 is seen in the workshop of the Experimental Department in early 1954. Behind it sits C-type XKC 012, fitted with disc brakes and louvered driver's door. *(LAT)*

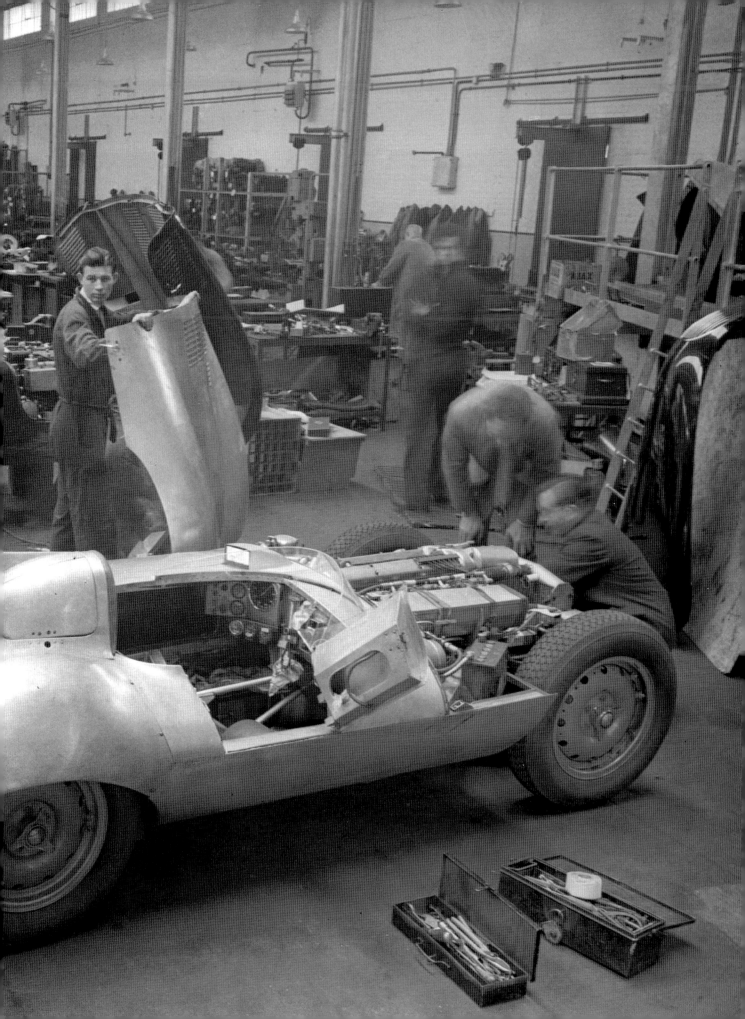

RIGHT The heart of a
D-type is its chassis,
or front subframe,
seen here with the
additional subframe
that supports the
radiator (yet to be
attached). *(Author)*

Chassis or front subframe

AD-type was legally identified by Jaguar
Cars by its chassis number, which
was stamped on to the frame, and it's this
component of the car that forms its main part,
rather than the monocoque centre section,
which simply carried the body number.

This chassis, or front subframe as it is
sometimes called, was initially made from
aluminium alloy on the first six D-types

constructed in 1954. However, for all
subsequent models the frame was constructed
from steel tubing of different cross-sections,
welded together and bolted, rather than
welded, to the monocoque, as this facilitated
easier repairs. The steel frame was extended
through the monocoque to the rear bulkhead
and served the purposes of attaching the
steering, suspension and brakes, supporting
and securing the engine and serving as a
transmission tunnel through the centre of the
monocoque to the rear axle.

The frame consists of a V-shaped or
arrowhead section, the ends of which bolt on
to the front bulkhead at either side. The front of
this arrowhead meets the rest of the subframe
at its front section, which is where the front
suspension (independent with torsion bars),
wheels, steering and radiator are attached.
The engine and gearbox are located in the
centre of the frame. This tapering rectangular-
shaped spaceframe then runs back through
the centre of the monocoque section to the
rear frame. In the event of frontal damage, the
radiator subframe can be removed by undoing
four bolts, while the entire chassis can also be
detached from the monocoque with ease.

Aircraft industry influence is shown in the
mounting of the engine. Five mounting points

BELOW The 'V' or
arrowhead on the front
of the frame can be
clearly seen here. The
bracket on the floor
supports the radiator.
(Author)

LEFT AND BELOW
The steel chassis is bolted to the front of the monocoque and runs through the centre to the rear. *(Author)*

BELOW The welded aluminium chassis of 1954 car XKD 406. Note the chassis number stamped on the frame. *(Author)*

BELOW Note the use of 'Oddie' nuts – a special type of locking nut used in period – to attach the frame to the front of the monocoque. *(Author)*

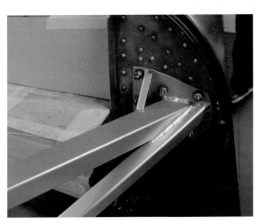

are used, two at the front and two at the rear with a fifth at the back of the gearbox. The two at the front are located so that loads on the mountings are transferred straight into the front suspension, on a shared part of the structure rather than being attached to separate parts of the chassis frame. 'It's rigidly mounted,' explained Chris Keith-Lucas, 'albeit, as Jaguar always would do, it was always on metalastic bushes, because they absolutely believed in insulating the car from the engine and the suspension.

'If you look at something like an XK,' he continued, 'you've a ladder chassis in effect, and then they found places to which they could bolt the suspension and engine. The two are

then quite a long way apart, so you need a lot of strength in the chassis. However, with the D-type there's a very short load path from the engine to the suspension and thus the whole frame can be pared down to a lighter set-up. You can even see that between the C-type, which was going that way, and the D-type. They don't quite bolt the suspension to the engine – that came later in Formula One – but it's getting very close, and the closer you can put them the less heavy a structure needs to go between them.'

Front suspension

Independent front suspension was used on the D-type, with upper and lower wishbones and longitudinal torsion bars. The D-type was designed with positive camber built in to counteract the back stepping out, in order to give neutral handling.

The top wishbone front rubber bushes are conical while the rears are parallel. 'The metalastic bushes are tapered and go in from either side,' explained Chris Keith-Lucas. 'They're located by the front one, which is two cones opposed, but the back one is a plain bush that can slide backwards and forwards. That way they're not fighting each other. It's a very clever design, and it's machined eccentrically, so by twisting the top spindle you can adjust the camber, and the thread allows you to adjust the castor. That winds the top wishbone forwards and backwards to give you the required castor angle.'

The same principle applies on the lower wishbone. The front bushes locate it, the back bush floats so that you're not straining the chassis when you tighten them up.

ABOVE LEFT The top nearside wishbone is offered up to its mounting on the front frame. *(Author)*

ABOVE The top wishbone in place. *(Author)*

ABOVE The lower wishbone has also now been fitted. *(Author)*

LEFT Close-up view of the adjustment for castor. *(Author)*

Each torsion bar, both front and rear, has 24 splines on the front and 25 on the rear. This uneven number allows the bar to be used as its own vernier to provide fine adjustment of the ride height. The number of possibilities of how the bar is fitted is therefore 24 x 25 = 600, and with all these options, as the bar is moved round one tooth at a time, one big gap forward and one slightly smaller gap back gives a great range of angles that can be subdivided for setting the ride height.

Chris Keith-Lucas explains the ride-height setting procedure: 'A setting bar which allows us to set the ride height is fitted instead of the shock absorber. The original D-type service manual gives you a setting-bar length, which you put there instead of a shock absorber and then set up the verniers so they all slide together correctly. In theory that will give you the correct ride height. In practice it almost never

LEFT Almost complete nearside front suspension, with wishbones, upright and steering arm in place. (*Author*)

BELOW LEFT The complete offside front suspension in place, showing the top wishbone and mountings, steering arm, brake caliper and disc. The only components yet to be attached are the Girling dampers. (*Author*)

BELOW Offside front suspension and steering in position. Note the setting bar in position in place of the shock absorber. (*Author*)

Central monocoque

The function of the monocoque was to provide a protective enclosure for the driver and passenger. It incorporates foot wells on each side, seat backs, and cut-outs in the upper surface.

Elliptical in cross-section, the monocoque comprises a stressed skin structure made from riveted sheet 16swg aluminium alloy, with front and rear bulkheads to provide rigidity and to locate the tubular front subframe, or chassis, which supports the engine and other components. A tapering gap in the floor accommodates this frame, which runs from front to back. The rear bulkhead also locates the rear frame.

Additional rigidity is provided by the bulkhead and the side sills, or pontoons, which run along each side of the tub. The front bulkhead sits on top of these pontoons, the lower half enclosing the driver's and passenger's foot well. Because of the way that the exhaust manifold was routed the passenger foot well is very short, whereas the driver has plenty of space. The foot well incorporates a 12swg bracket for mounting the brake master cylinder and brackets for the clutch and brake pedals.

Initially the car had a single driver's door, made from 18swg. In the earlier cars this was

ABOVE Girling damper in position between the cross-member and lower wishbone. *(CKL)*

does, mainly because we're running lower ride heights these days than we were in period.'

Girling type CDR 4½ telescopic dampers are used in both front and rear suspensions. At the front, these are attached to the upper section of the front cross-member at the top and the lower wishbone at the bottom, whilst rears are inclined transversely to clear the upper suspension links.

RIGHT The front of the central monocoque, or cockpit section, of the D-type Jaguar. The tape is to protect the polished front surface of the bulkhead. *(Author)*

RIGHT The back of the front bulkhead showing the aperture for the steering column, which is adjustable, and the holes for various cables to the speedometer and tachometer.
(Author)

18.5in long, but it was increased to 19.7in and a passenger door fitted in order to comply with the Appendix C regulations that came into force for 1957.

Constructed mainly of sheets of 16swg aluminium, the central monocoque's elliptical shape provides good torsional rigidity and its small cross-section helps reduce drag. The front bulkhead sits atop the two side sills, or pontoons, which run front to back.

The rear bulkhead closes off the end of the monocoque and acts as a firewall between the cockpit and the fuel tank, as well as providing rigidity. Two parallel 12swg channels run across the rear bulkhead, attached to the pontoons, seat backs and lower skin by multiple rivets. These are used to locate the rear suspension, subframe and the tail, along with the fuel tank.

RIGHT The rear bulkhead can be clearly seen in this view of the back end of the monocoque.
(Author)

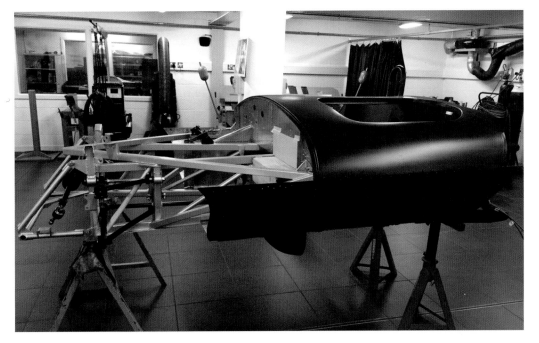

LEFT The painted monocoque with the front subframe, or chassis, attached. Note that there was no passenger door on the pre-1957 models. Instead a detachable tonneau cover was fitted over the oval aperture above the passenger seat.
(Author)

Cutaway of Jaguar D-type.

(Tony Matthews)

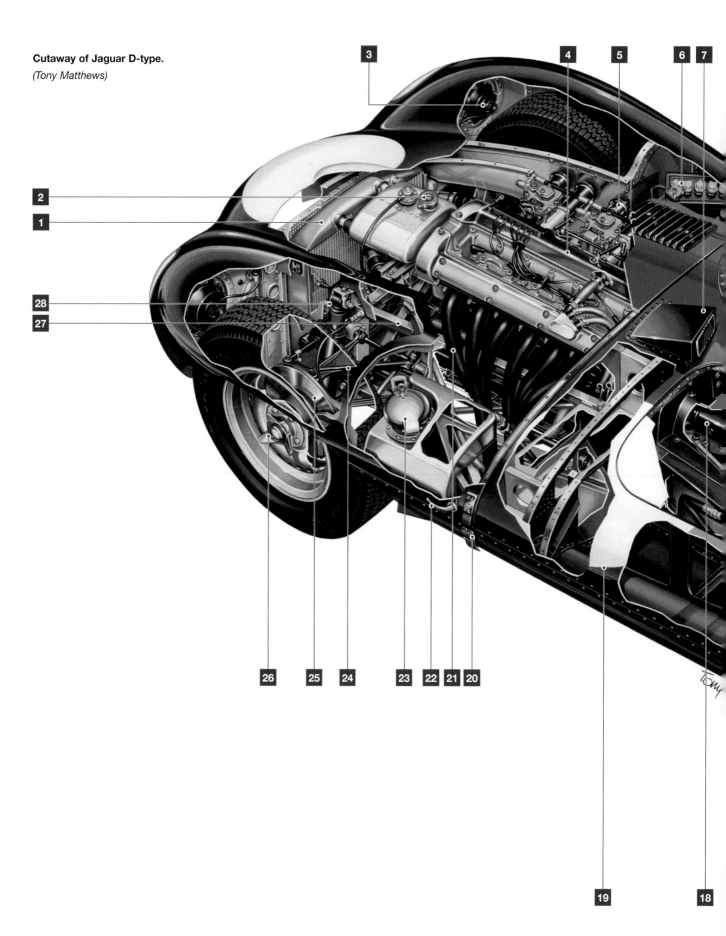

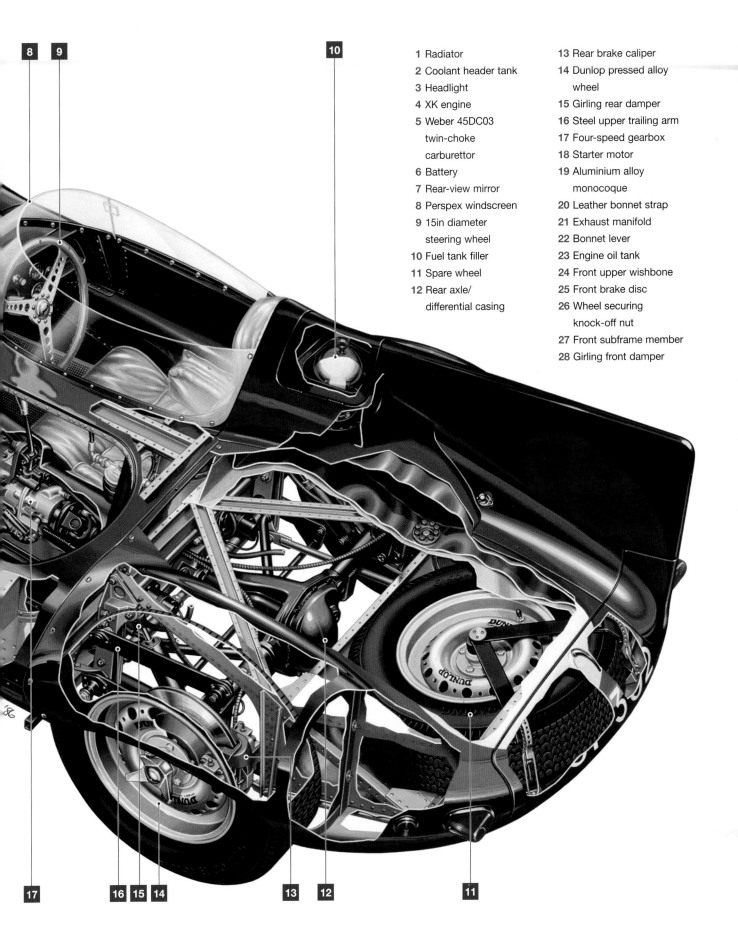

1 Radiator
2 Coolant header tank
3 Headlight
4 XK engine
5 Weber 45DC03 twin-choke carburettor
6 Battery
7 Rear-view mirror
8 Perspex windscreen
9 15in diameter steering wheel
10 Fuel tank filler
11 Spare wheel
12 Rear axle/differential casing
13 Rear brake caliper
14 Dunlop pressed alloy wheel
15 Girling rear damper
16 Steel upper trailing arm
17 Four-speed gearbox
18 Starter motor
19 Aluminium alloy monocoque
20 Leather bonnet strap
21 Exhaust manifold
22 Bonnet lever
23 Engine oil tank
24 Front upper wishbone
25 Front brake disc
26 Wheel securing knock-off nut
27 Front subframe member
28 Girling front damper

Rear frame and suspension

The four-part rear subframe of the D-type is descended from the rear section of the C-type, being constructed from folded upright steel sections with a torsion bar tube. Its sole purpose is to attach the rear axle and suspension to the rest of the car.

The rear suspension is by means of trailing links with a solid rear axle and a single transverse torsion bar. This is enclosed in the torsion bar tube at the bottom of the rear frame and has an enlarged centre section that's anchored at the centre of the tube, effectively producing two torsion bars acting independently.

The rear fabricated steel subframe is bolted to the rear bulkhead of the monocoque and supports the trailing arms and shock absorbers of the rear suspension. The lower longitudinal tube is hollow and contains the torsion bar, while the upper one just acts as a spacer, keeping the upright sections of the frame the correct distance apart. These days it's often used for the attachment of seat belts. As with the front suspension, the ride height is adjusted by vernier splined sleeves at the ends of the torsion bar.

CENTRE Overall view of the rear bulkhead with small rear subframe and part of the rear suspension attached. Note that the roll hoop shown wasn't standard in period but is favoured by many D-type owners for competition use today. *(Author)*

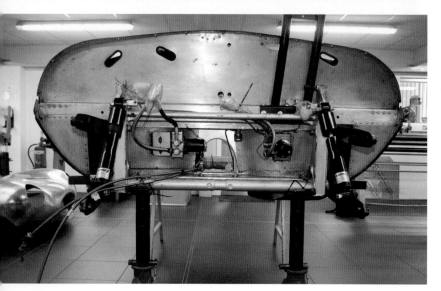

LEFT The opening for the transmission can clearly be seen in this view of the rear bulkhead, and the single torsion bar was housed in the large diameter tube below it. The narrow middle section of the tube is where the square centre-section of the torsion bar is anchored, allowing it to effectively act as two separate torsion bars. *(Author)*

The live rear axle is carried on a pair of trailing steel arms on each side. The arms are made from sprung steel with metalastic bushes in the ends, which allow movement when the car rolls. 'There are no rose joints on a D-type,' explained Chris Keith-Lucas, 'as they hadn't come into motor racing at this time. But if you look at racing cars from just a couple of years later, they're used extensively. They were already used at this time in the aircraft industry as rod ends for control linkages and things like that, but not on Jaguars.'

An A-frame runs from either side of the rear frame to a rotating joint under the centre of the rear axle, centralising it.

As well as the large A-frame, a smaller,

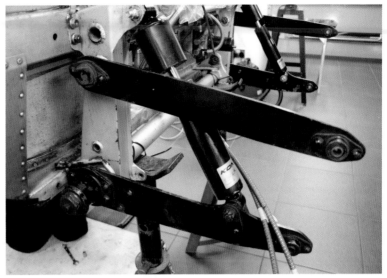

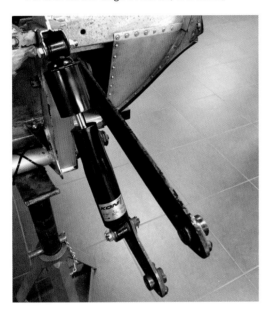

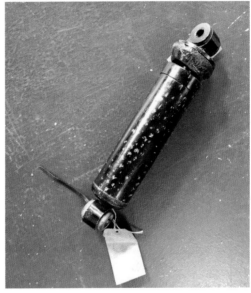

ABOVE The live rear axle was carried on the trailing steel arms seen here, with the lower ends of the shock absorbers attached to the lower steel arms. *(Author)*

FAR LEFT The (non-period) shock absorbers were inclined transversely to clear the upper suspension links. *(Author)*

ABOVE A period Girling type CDR 4½ shock absorber. *(Author)*

LEFT The right-hand A-frame mounting on the fabricated steel frame. *(Author)*

BELOW The small secondary A-frame that fitted under the differential. *(John Pearson collection)*

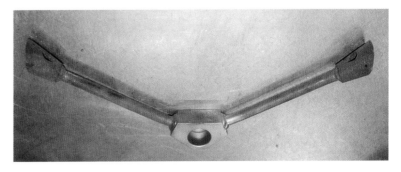

ABOVE The trailing arms supported the solid rear axle and brakes, while the lower A-frame centralised the solid rear axle. *(Author)*

ABOVE RIGHT The trailing arms were manufactured in sprung steel and are therefore able to absorb twist when the car rolls. *(Author)*

RIGHT A complete rear end with suspension and transmission in place, the propshaft pointing through the hole in the rear bulkhead. *(Author)*

BELOW The complete rear end with period Girling shock absorbers fitted. *(CKL)*

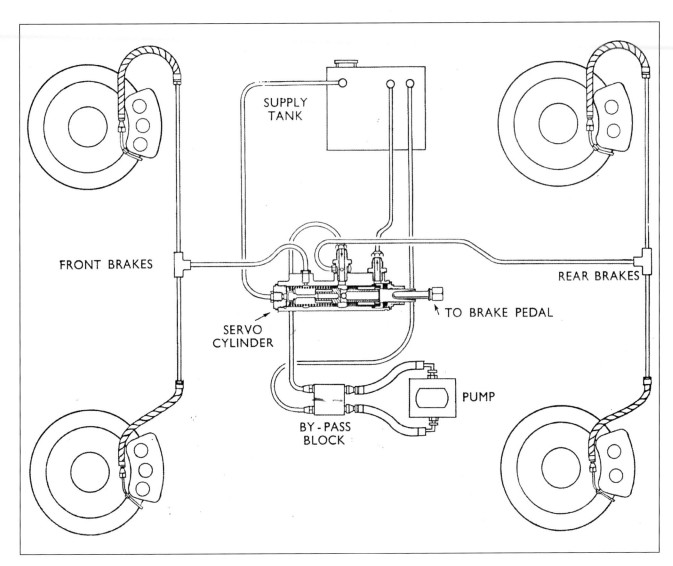

FRONT BRAKES

SUPPLY TANK

REAR BRAKES

SERVO CYLINDER

TO BRAKE PEDAL

BY-PASS BLOCK

PUMP

secondary one sits underneath the differential, the two being connected by a pin providing a low roll-centre for the car.

Brakes

The D-type is fitted all round with 12¾in diameter Dunlop disc brakes made from chromium-plated mild steel, with six pot calipers on the front and four pots on the rear, giving a 60/40 split in brake effort from front to back, which isn't adjustable. It has 20 Mintex pads, 12 front and 8 rear. A dual hydraulic system operates the brakes with servo assistance from a Plessey pump driven from the back of the gearbox.

The Plessey pump is used to provide hydraulic pressure to push the pads on to the discs. It's driven off the transmission, so that at low speed it provides hardly any braking, but at high speed

the brakes could have a tendency to lock up. At that point the transmission stops going round and there's no pressure and no brakes at all.

A master cylinder acts on the front brakes only, while at the same time distributing the pressure from the fluid flowing from the Plessey pump to both front and rear brakes. A larger, baffled reservoir next to the master cylinder cools and de-aerates the circulating fluid. When the car is reversing, of course, the Plessey pump runs backwards and so a bypass valve closes off the system, leaving only the front brakes to operate when the car is in reverse. On the 1954 cars and all production cars the systems were separate, so that in the event of a failure of the Plessey-powered system the driver would still retain some braking capability.

A disadvantage of this dual system is the locking-up problem mentioned above. 'It means

ABOVE **Diagram of the servo system taken from the 'Dunlop Disc Brake Maintenance Notes' of the period.** *(John Pearson Collection)*

it's more difficult to modulate the pressure accurately on the rear brakes,' explained Gary Pearson, 'which is why they're prone to locking up.' As a result, for 1955 and 1956 the works and works-prepared cars (which meant those running at Le Mans including the Ecurie Francorchamps, Ecurie Ecosse and Border Reivers cars) had what was called the Full Pressure or Full Power system, which provided the servo-assisted braking on the front as well as the rears. It did mean, though, that if the Plessey pump failed, without the hydraulic assistance the brakes would be fairly ineffective at racing speeds, or, as Chris Keith-Lucas put it: 'If it goes wrong, it goes wrong big time...'

The cast iron master cylinder of the braking system acts as a servo, with the proportioning mechanism to distribute the fluid front and rear inside the cylinder. 'The whole braking system on these cars is fairly unique because it was the world's first and they were experimenting to see

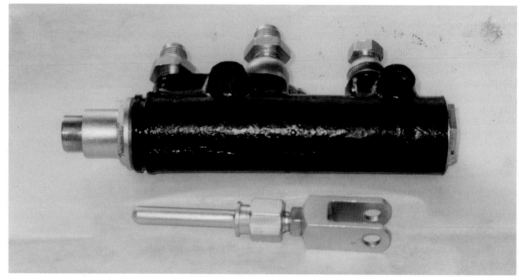

RIGHT Dunlop brake master cylinder as fitted to 1954 works and 1955–56 customer cars. (John Pearson collection)

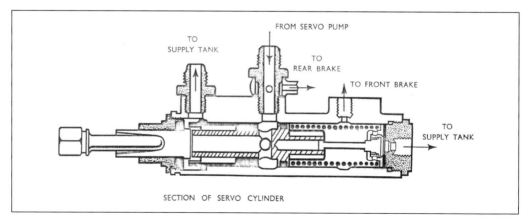

RIGHT Section through master cylinder for servo system. (CKL)

RIGHT The black cylindrical brake hydraulic
fluid reservoir on the bulkhead, with the cast-
iron master cylinder mounted next to it. The
master cylinder pushrod isn't attached in this
photograph. *(Author)*

the best way of making it operate,' explained
Chris. 'They did find simpler ways of doing it
later on. The idea that it needed a hydraulic
pressure supply probably came from the aircraft
background of the people that were developing
that system and later on, obviously, we've
discovered that disc brakes can be worked
perfectly well with a conventional master
cylinder. But at that time they thought that it
was a good idea to have hydraulic pressure
available, driven by a Plessey pump driven off
the back of the transmission, so you've got
quite a complicated system for working that.'

The master cylinder input piston which
is pushed back when the driver brakes is
activated by the pushrod from the end of the
pedal, which pivots. When the driver pushes the
pedal forward, the top of the pedal comes back
above the pivot, pushes the pushrod inwards
and applies the brakes.

The front calipers have six pistons. Originally
the discs were covered in a thick layer of hard
chrome to improve their wear characteristics
when very hot. 'Each brake piston has two
retractor pins that pull it back off the disc,

BELOW Compare this photograph with the one above. This shows the alloy
master cylinder (as opposed to the cast iron version) of the Full Pressure
system. Whereas the standard system has three pipes connected to it, the
FP system only has two, since it doesn't incorporate an independent system
for the front brakes, so the front section of the tank is blanked off. *(Author)*

BELOW Front disc brake with six-pot calipers
and conventional bleed nipple at the top. The
'LF' on the caliper shows that it is the left front.
(Author)

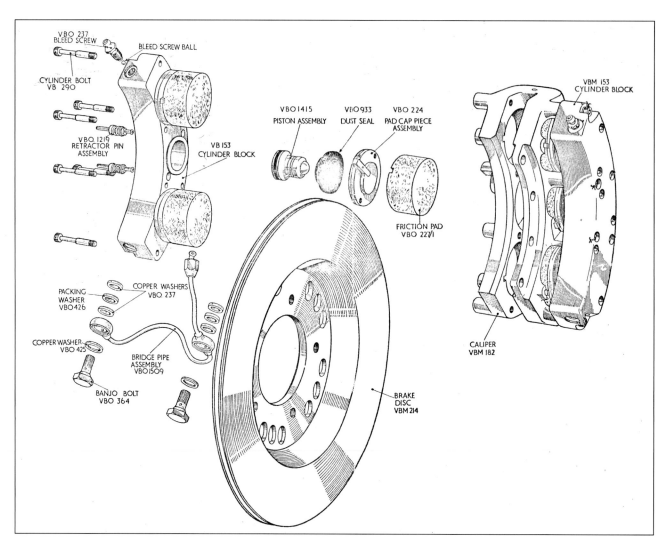

VBO 237
BLEED SCREW

BLEED SCREW BALL

CYLINDER BOLT
VB 290

VBO 1219
RETRACTOR PIN
ASSEMBLY

VB 153
CYLINDER BLOCK

VBO 1415
PISTON ASSEMBLY

VBO 933
DUST SEAL

VBO 224
PAD CAP PIECE
ASSEMBLY

FRICTION PAD
VBO 227/1

VBM 153
CYLINDER BLOCK

PACKING
WASHER
VBO 426

COPPER WASHERS
VBO 237

COPPER WASHER
VBO 425

BRIDGE PIPE
ASSEMBLY
VBO 1509

BANJO BOLT
VBO 364

BRAKE
DISC
VBM 214

CALIPER
VBM 182

ABOVE Diagram showing detail of the six-pot front brakes on the D-type.
(John Pearson collection)

explained Chris. 'Actually, if they work too well they're a complete pain; you're almost better off without them. In the early days of disc brake development it was thought essential that the pads have a withdrawal system. Later on it was discovered that the brake seal has a little bit of that tendency anyway, in that they've got a bit of spring in them so that when you push them on they shove the piston to the disc, but when you take the hydraulic pressure off, the rubber springs back and actually performs that function for you. But that wasn't known in those days.

'Each pad is something like an inch and a quarter thick,' he continued, 'so there's a massive amount of available wear. The intention wasn't to make a brake on which it was easy to change the pads, but rather a brake that

would last a whole 24 hours of racing without the need to change pads. Which is just as well, because it's actually a really long job to put new pads in a D-type. It can take eight hours a corner if you're not careful – it's a huge job. To change the pads you really have to totally strip the brake. So they used a completely different set of assumptions and said, "Right, we've got to make a brake that's going to last 24 hours without any maintenance." A very clever way of doing it. Later on the works D-types did evolve a quick-change brake with a smaller pad, which was probably slightly less effective but which could be changed quickly.'

The handbrake mechanism on the rear four-pot caliper locates in the back plate. 'All machined from solid bits,' said Chris. 'And that's where you begin to see why the D-type was such an expensive car to build.'

The bypass/reversing valve short-circuits

FAR LEFT The rigid bridge pipe assembly runs from side to side underneath the caliper and is located by silver-soldered banjo bolts at each end. Nowadays owners tend to use modern Aeroquip flexible pipes. *(CKL)*

ABOVE LEFT Front upright and steering arm assembly with brake caliper. *(Author)*

FAR LEFT Complete front upright and brake assembly. *(Author)*

LEFT This close-up of a front caliper shows the six pistons. *(Author)*

FAR LEFT Later quick-change brake with smaller pads. *(CKL)*

LEFT Rear four-pot caliper assembly showing the flexible interconnecting pipe between the caliper halves, and the handbrake mechanism. *(Author)*

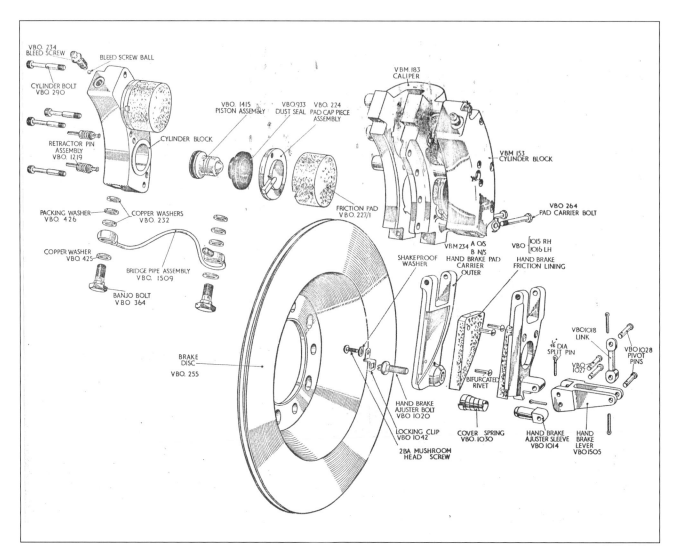

VBO. 234
BLEED SCREW

BLEED SCREW BALL

CYLINDER BOLT
VBO. 290

RETRACTOR PIN
ASSEMBLY
VBO. 1219

VBO. 1415
PISTON ASSEMBLY

VBO.933
DUST SEAL

VBO. 224
PAD CAP PIECE
ASSEMBLY

CYLINDER BLOCK

VBM. 183
CALIPER

VBM 153
CYLINDER BLOCK

VBO 264
PAD CARRIER BOLT

PACKING WASHER
VBO. 426

COPPER WASHERS
VBO. 232

COPPER WASHER
VBO. 425

BRIDGE PIPE ASSEMBLY
VBO. 1509

BANJO BOLT
VBO. 364

FRICTION PAD
VBO. 227/1

VBM 234 A O/S
B N/S

VBO 1015 RH
1016 LH

SHAKEPROOF
WASHER

HAND BRAKE PAD
CARRIER
OUTER

HAND BRAKE
FRICTION LINING

VBO1018
LINK

VBO 1028
PIVOT
PINS

1/16 DIA
SPLIT PIN

VBO
1027

BRAKE
DISC
VBO. 255

BIFURCATED
RIVET

HAND BRAKE
AJUSTER BOLT
VBO 1020

LOCKING CLIP
VBO 1042

2BA MUSHROOM
HEAD SCREW

COVER SPRING
VBO. 1030

HAND BRAKE
AJUSTER SLEEVE
VBO 1014

HAND
BRAKE
LEVER
VBO 1505

ABOVE Diagram showing detail of the four-pot rear brakes. *(John Pearson collection)*

LEFT The rear nearside disc brake with four-pot caliper. *(Author)*

BELOW Rear offside disc with four-pot caliper and bleed nipple at the top. *(Author)*

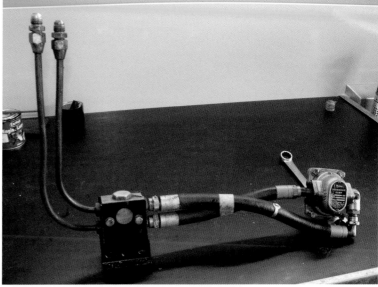

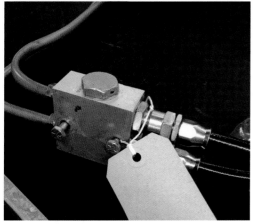

ABOVE LEFT Rear four-pot brake caliper. *(Author)*

ABOVE The Plessey pump which pressurises the hydraulic braking system, together with the reversing valve. *(CKL)*

LEFT The Plessey pump in situ. *(CKL)*

ABOVE The bypass/reversing valve short-circuits the Plessey pump, stopping the brake-fluid flow if the car is reversing. *(Author)*

the Plessey pump, stopping the flow of the brake fluid in the system in the event of the car reversing. The flexible pipes shown in the picture aren't original. 'The reversing valve is a key component,' explained Chris, 'because when the car is reversing, the brake pressure pump – the Plessey pump – starts to run backwards. And if you didn't have that valve you'd theoretically put your foot on the brakes and suck the pads away from the disc. So when the car is going backwards this bypass valve opens and the brake fluid is purely pumped back into itself through that valve, in a closed loop. And that's a very, very important little invention.'

LEFT The two pipes come up from the Plessey pump, drawing brake fluid from the reservoir and pumping it back under pressure. The fluid is constantly circulating and the driver taps into that pressure when he puts his foot on the brake pedal. *(Author)*

RIGHT Handbrake cable connected to handbrake mechanism on rear brake. (*Author*)

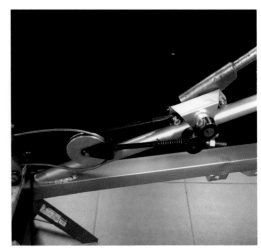

FAR RIGHT The handbrake mechanism inside the cockpit. (*Author*)

BELOW Alternative view of handbrake mechanism inside cockpit. (*Author*)

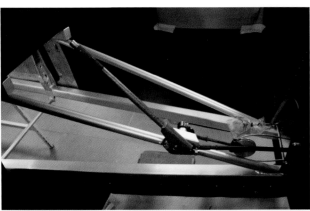

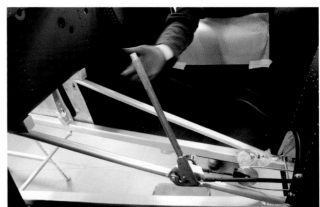

ABOVE RIGHT Demonstrating the fly-off mechanism. To release the handbrake, the lever merely has to be flipped upwards. (*Author*)

RIGHT The handbrake mechanism, together with a modern equivalent Plessey pump that will be bolted to the gearbox when installed. Also visible to the right is the reversing valve that short-circuits the hydraulic braking system when the car is put into reverse. (*Author*)

Handbrake

The handbrake incorporates a quick release or 'fly-off' mechanism, which means the driver only has to flick the lever up to release it. 'To operate the handbrake you just pull on it and then press the tit and the handbrake stays there,' explained John Pearson of Pearsons Engineering, 'and this is where people go wrong. Starting off with the handbrake on (I never used to put the handbrake on – they never work anyway!), you don't press the tit, you just ease the lever back and it goes "ping". It's called a fly-off handbrake. Pre-war cars used to have that, and it's sprung, so you let the brake off and the cable rewinds.'

Steering

Steering on the D-type is by conventional rack and pinion. The steering arm runs parallel with the wishbones to prevent bump steer. The steering rack was manufactured in a similar way to that of the XK140 and XK150 cars but with different brackets and some other minor differences, so was almost a production item on the car but not directly interchangeable. The track rod ends were made by a company known as A&A, or Alford and Alder, of Hemel Hempstead.

LEFT The pinion housing was located at the far right-hand end of the rack housing. *(Author)*

LEFT A track rod end. Note the grease nipple on the top of the ball joint. *(Author)*

LEFT The unique Mollart coupling universal joint in the steering column. *(Author)*

BELOW The complete rack-and-pinion steering assembly attached to the front subframe. *(Author)*

LEFT Steering assembly, upper and lower wishbones, torsion bar, brakes and wheel in place. *(Author)*

CENTRE The upper end of the steering column. This photograph is of an XKSS undergoing restoration. *(John Pearson collection)*

The universal joint in the steering column is an unusual type called a Mollart coupling, which wasn't seen on any other car. It consists of two pincers surrounding a central ball that has two longitudinal grooves cut into it at 90° to each other, like lines of longitude and latitude, allowing the whole assembly to move around the ball. 'If you slide it all together at a certain angle, then straighten it out, everything locks up and you can't pull it apart, making it very strong,' said Chris Keith-Lucas. 'By necessity, they always have a certain amount of play in them or else they wouldn't work, which can be a bit of a pain, but that's normal for a D-type. Why they particularly liked that coupling for that application I don't know. It's not on any other Jaguar.'

The steering column is splined at its upper end to receive the wheel and is supported by two 'Tufnol' spherical self-aligning bearings located on the upper tube.

The steering column assembly comprises two short tubes, connected by a universal joint at the point where it passes through the wall of the pedal compartment. Another universal joint then connects the column assembly to the pinion shaft at the steering box.

RIGHT The steering column in situ in the chassis, showing the two tubes and the universal joint. *(Author)*

LEFT AND BELOW
The tail with its
distinctive fin. *(Author)*

Bodywork

Tail

T he aluminium-magnesium alloy tail is
secured to the monocoque by four ⅜in
main bolts, plus a series of mushroom-headed
2BA screws securing the top panelling. It has
no internal framework but consists of a stressed
18swg aluminium skin structure with internal
diaphragms to provide stiffness. Spot-welded
within the tail is the 16swg fuel tank, which
contains a Marston Aviation Division rubber
bag tank. This had a capacity of 36.5 gallons
(166 litres) and in the original design, a main
and supplementary tank was specified but this
was replaced by a single tank in the production
D-type.

From inside the boot it's possible to access
the cover plate of the nut rings, or stud rings
as they're sometimes called, which hold the
flexible fuel tank to the fuel tank cell. Another
four are located underneath the car and
another one on top of the filler neck case.
According to Chris Keith-Lucas, making the
seal is always a drama. 'There's so many
ways that it can leak,' he explained, 'because
the fuel can capillary out through the threads,

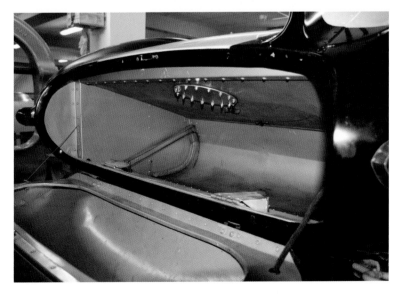

**RIGHT Looking inside the boot it's possible to
see the cover plate of the nut rings, or stud rings,
that hold the flexible fuel tank to the fuel tank
cell.** *(Author)*

RIGHT The unpainted nose section of the car is placed next to the complete tail unit. *(Author)*

and it's a very unusual D-type if, when you open the spare wheel compartment, you don't get a tiny whiff of petrol. They're almost impossible to totally seal, but it's only a minute amount of leakage and from a safety point of view that's acceptable.'

Bonnet

The bonnet of the D-type is made from an 18swg aluminium skin with 16swg internals. It includes ducting for the carburettors and, on the later long-nose cars, for the brakes as well. The longer nose of the 1955 works cars added 7½in to their overall length.

The underside of the noses on both the works C- and D-types at Le Mans were painted silver to reflect the light when working on the cars at night.

The following step-by-step photograph sequence shows how a replacement bonnet is crafted from aluminium at CKL Developments.

RIGHT The exhaust cowling on the bottom of the bodywork. This is the point at which the pipes will exit through the body when they've been fitted. *(Author)*

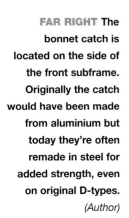

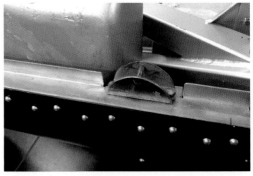

FAR RIGHT The bonnet catch is located on the side of the front subframe. Originally the catch would have been made from aluminium but today they're often remade in steel for added strength, even on original D-types. *(Author)*

RIGHT Rear view of D-type inside the workshops of CKL Developments. *(Author)*

ABOVE CKL Developments director Chris Keith-Lucas with the fibreglass 'buck' that's used to form a replacement bonnet for a D-type. Aluminium sections are shaped using a wheeling machine before being checked over the buck and welded together, the welds then being gently hammered smooth. (*Author*)

ABOVE RIGHT The individual panels that will form the nose are marked out on the buck and numbered. (*Author*)

RIGHT The replacement aluminium bonnet, still in its 'raw' form, has been formed carefully into shape. (*Author*)

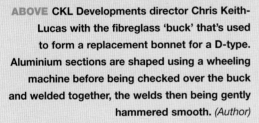

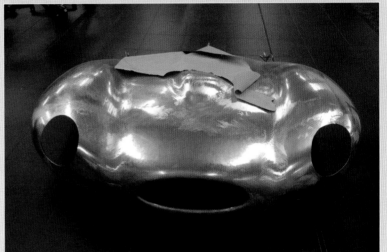

RIGHT Internal ducting, made from 16swg aluminium, channels air through the central opening to the radiator and oil cooler and, via the square-sectioned duct, to the carburettors. (*Author*)

BELOW Apertures are cut for the headlights. (*Author*)

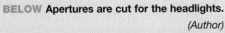

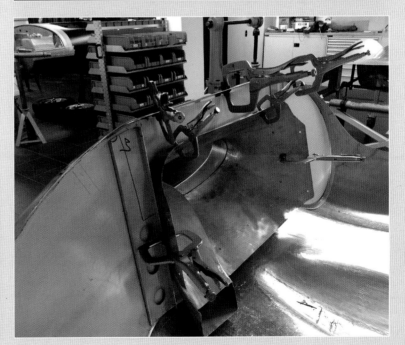

ABOVE The bonnet with internal ducting attached and louvres cut is moved into place. *(Author)*

ABOVE The long duct on the left feeds air directly to the square-section airbox over the Weber carburettors, bypassing the radiator. This allows the carburettors to drink cold, dense air rather than hot, already expanded air that's passed through the radiator, thus producing the best volumetric efficiency. *(Author)*

RIGHT The level of detail in the design of the D-type is illustrated by the special bolt that holds the bonnet hinge pin together, with its flat head and two milled flats. *(Author)*

FAR RIGHT Bonnet bolt in position. *(Author)*

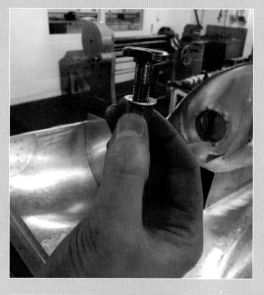

RIGHT The bonnet is now attached to the front frame and the front suspension can be seen through the headlamp aperture. *(Author)*

FAR RIGHT Internal ducting being attached to the bonnet. *(Author)*

BELOW FAR LEFT
The radiator grille and ducting. The air intake goes from oval in the mouth of the nose to square and air is fed from the nose through the square ducting to the carburettors. Alongside is the spreader/stiffener that holds the bottom hinge and spreads the stresses through the front bulkhead. (*Author*)

LEFT The spreader/stiffener also serves as a flange to which captive nuts are attached. These are used to retain the internal air duct, which is made removable so that any crash damage can be tapped out from the inside. The captive 2BA nuts, which are of Second World War aircraft origin, contain a friction device that prevents the 2BA bolts from falling out, even if they become loose. (*Author*)

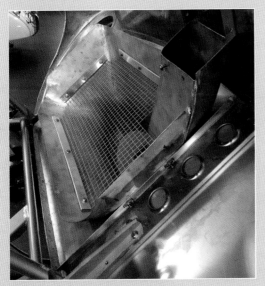

ABOVE Replacement bonnet is in position, attached to the front subframe. *(Author)*

ABOVE RIGHT Inside view of the unpainted replacement bonnet. *(Author)*

RIGHT Cooling louvres cut in bonnet. *(Author)*

ABOVE The replacement bonnet is sanded down prior to being sent for painting. *(Author)*

BELOW LEFT In the workshops of Kingswell Coachworks, the bonnet is filled and shaped with a layer of polyester liquid filler before being finely sanded down to a smooth finish. *(Author)*

BELOW The louvres on the bonnet are given special attention. *(Author)*

FAR LEFT In the paint shop, the bonnet is ready for its first coat of black primer to be applied. *(Author)*

LEFT Black is used to match the colour of the final coat so that any stone chipping caused when driving won't show up. *(Author)*

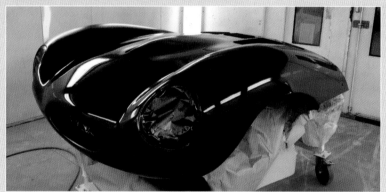

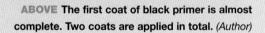

ABOVE The first coat of black primer is almost complete. Two coats are applied in total. *(Author)*

ABOVE RIGHT With two coats of primer applied, the bonnet is almost ready for its top coats. *(Author)*

RIGHT The two coats of primer are carefully rubbed down, or 'flattened', prior to the final top coats being applied. *(Author)*

BELOW The rubbed down primer is now ready for the top coat. *(Author)*

BELOW The final stage is the application of three top coats of paint, which is left for five minutes and then baked at 70°C for half an hour. *(Author)*

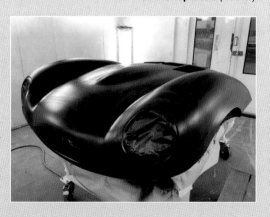

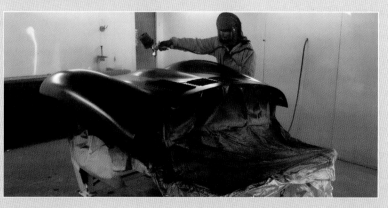

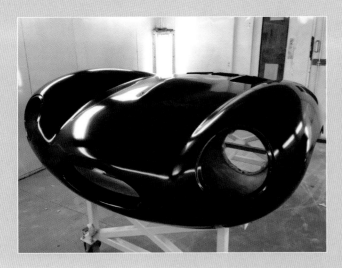

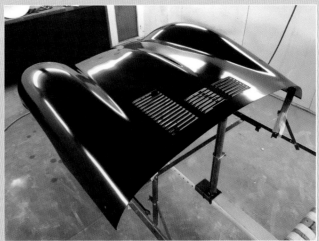

ABOVE AND ABOVE RIGHT The finished product.
(Nigel Baker)

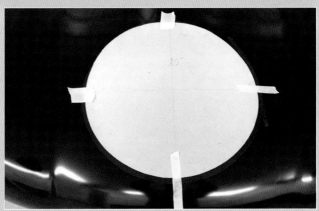

RIGHT AND BELOW The final task is to mask the paint
for the roundel to be applied. *(Nigel Baker)*

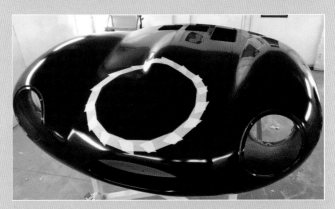

Engine

The engine of the D-type was based on Jaguar's production 3½ litre, inline six-cylinder XK block, producing 246bhp, but modified in the way it was attached to the gearbox and bellhousing so that it was inclined at an angle of 8½° to the left when viewed from the cockpit. This was to aid installation, and the barrels of the three twin-choke Weber carburettors are also inclined at the same angle so that they lie horizontal when the engine is installed. The engine is coupled to a four-speed synchromesh gearbox and a triple dry-plate clutch.

The cylinder block and crankcase are formed from a single iron casting with the bores machined direct into the casting. The bores are relatively long, giving a bore to stroke ratio of 0.778:1. The engine has no flywheel, but a crankshaft torsional vibration damper at the front. The flywheel effect is achieved by the mass of the triple-plate clutch and its housing, along with the starter ring, which is bolted on

to the clutch assembly. An 8¼in adaptor plate allows direct fitting of the Borg & Beck clutch.

The light alloy cylinder head is a revised version of that seen on the last C-types, with hemispherical combustion chambers and inclined valves with dual overhead camshafts. The depth of the cylinder head was dictated by the need to allow room for large valves but not restrict the flow of gases, resulting in a relatively wide angle between the long-stem valves. Brico pistons gave a compression ratio of 9:1 and the conventional connecting rods, crankshaft and bearing caps were used, but all were specially prepared.

All the customer cars were fitted with the basic cylinder head at the time but this was replaced on the works cars from 1955 onwards by one with a slightly wider angle between the inlet and exhaust valves, with the latter being inclined by an extra 5°. 'If you went from a narrow angle to a wider angle, you could actually get slightly bigger valves in, without them tangling at high revs,' explained John Pearson. 'So the standard arrangement from

ABOVE Jaguar XK engine with wide-angle 35/40 head, as fitted to the works D-types from 1955 onwards. *(LAT)*

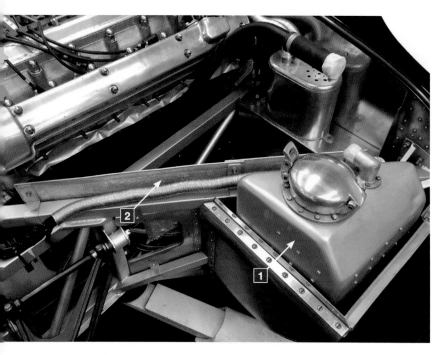

the beginning with the XK engine was a valve angle of 70° (35° and 35°). But the later head is 35° and 40° – another 5° – and is known as the wide-angled or 35/40 head.'

ABOVE **Triangular dry sump tank (1) and heat shield (2).** *(Author)*

Dry sump lubrication

The dry sump lubrication system was described in the original D-type service manual thus: 'The lubrication of the engine is carried out on the "dry sump" principle. Oil is drawn from the three-gallon return tank situated under the bonnet on the left-hand side of the car, by a gear pump located to the right-hand side of the engine. From thence it passes to an oil cooler, which is mounted on the right-hand side of the main water radiator. The oil is then directed to

BELOW **The dry sump tank on a production D-type.** *(Author)*

BELOW RIGHT **Oil tank on works Le Mans 3.8-litre car. Note the ring for the plombeur's seal** *(Author)*

a transfer block adjacent to the main engine oil gallery. After passing through the various bearings, the oil drains back to a shallow sump, from whence it is scavenged by a three-gear pump, mounted on the left-hand side of the engine, to the return tank. The return tank is vented to the crankcase via a large-diameter steel tube, flexibly connected to each by a long, oil-resistant hose. When replacing this hose, it is essential to see that the ends of the pipe do not butt on either tank or crankcase connections. Sufficient length of flexible pipe is provided for this purpose. A relief valve is provided in the pressure oil pump, and engine oil pressure is maintained by a pre-set spring. Normal running oil pressure is 45/50lb per sq in.'

With the dry sump system there's the requirement for an additional oil pump with drive taken from a gear between the front main bearing and the timing chain wheel. The crankshaft gear engages with the mating gear which drives a transverse shaft, operating the pressure pump on the right-hand side of the engine and the scavenge pump on the left-hand side.

The dry sump tank is triangular in cross-section in order to fit between the front subframe and the sill. The catch tank in the picture is a modern requirement. The asbestos/aluminium heat shield with the wiring loom running through a heatproof flexible pipe is the same as used in period.

Oil from the tank is drawn by pressure pump to the bottom of the oil cooler. It passes through this and along an external pipe to the crankcase, where it lubricates the bearings via internal drillings. Aeration of the oil is prevented

by baffles inside the tank, with a breather pipe running from the top of the tank, between the two exhaust manifolds, to the crankcase. The oil tank is situated behind the left front wheel, while the battery is in a similar position behind the right front wheel.

The works Le Mans cars had a different type of oil tank with an increased capacity, being taller and shaped around the cap, as can be seen on the 3.8-litre engine pictured. The tank was located in the same place but had a bigger space above to help de-aerate the oil more.

Engine variants

The XK engine came in a number of forms during the life of the D-type. The engine was first introduced in 1949 with an initial capacity of 3,442cc and was used in the XK120, 140, 150 and C-type before finding its way into the new D-type Jaguar in 1954. A short-block version of 2,483cc was introduced in 1955 and fitted to the Mk1 Jaguar saloon. This shorter block was used for 2.4- and 2.8-litre engines, while the full-sized block was used for the 3.4-, 3.8- and the much later 4.2-litre engines.

In 1958, new regulations meant that the D-types had to run with 3.0-litre engines. To achieve this Jaguar de-stroked the 3.4-litre unit, but it was never developed properly and proved to be unreliable. A 3.8-litre version of the engine was also released in 1958.

ABOVE The casting is where an oil filter would be located on a saloon car, but on the D-type none is fitted. *(Author)*

LEFT The XK engine awaiting installation. The exhaust apertures have been covered with masking tape for protection. *(Author)*

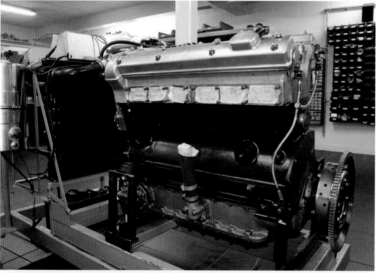

LEFT The dry sump pan is made in two sections, upper and lower. Normally the sump is just like a bathtub that bolts up to the bottom of the engine, but on the D-type it's in two sections bolted together. *(Author)*

OPPOSITE The 3.5-litre XK engine sits within the front subframe. *(Author)*

BELOW LEFT The pressure pump for the dry sump system, seen here, is located on one side of the engine, the scavenge pump on the other. *(Author)*

BELOW The front right-hand engine mounting viewed from above. *(Author)*

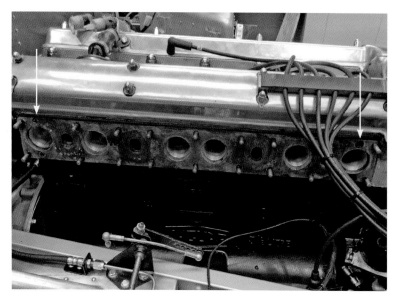

ABOVE The cylinder head to inlet manifold adaptor plate in place. Note the countersunk securing screws (arrowed). *(Author)*

BELOW The engine is canted over at an angle of 8½°. *(Author)*

Engine mountings

Aircraft industry influence was shown in the mounting of the engine. Five mounting points are used – two at the front, two at the rear and another at the back of the gearbox. The two at the front are located so that loads on the mountings are transferred straight into the front suspension, on a shared part of the structure rather than being attached to separate parts of the chassis frame.

Fuel and ignition systems

Between the cylinder head and the manifold is a steel adaptor plate that moves the stud positions, allowing the manifold to be bolted on. Because early head castings had studs directly below and above the port, which didn't allow a Weber carburettor manifold to be bolted on, the adaptor plate was used, as Chris Keith-Lucas explained: 'The adaptor plate did two things. One is that it helped port matching between the

head and the manifold; but more importantly it put the studs where you actually needed to have them, and it's attached to the head with countersunk bolts, which are only just visible.' It's only the two front and two rear studs that the adaptor plate relocated, moving them outwards, the others remaining in the same place.

D-types originally used 45DC03 Weber carburettors. 'Dunlop Aviation made all the fuel pipe fittings for the car,' explained Chris, 'so they're all much, much higher quality. There's no jubilee clips and bits of pushed-on hose or stuff like that, they're all beautiful aircraft swaged fittings – a huge bit of overkill for something where the fuel pressure is only a couple of psi, but nevertheless, absolutely reliable and all done for reliability.'

An intake duct in the bonnet draws air from the radiator grille to an open-ended box that surrounds the carburettor intakes (not shown) and eliminates the need for pressure balancing pipes to the float chambers.

An interesting feature of the D-type engine is the plug lead separator fitted to the right-hand cam cover. 'These are much imitated, but in fact they really only ever appeared on the D-type in period,' said Chris. 'On the saloon cars they used to pack the leads into a sort of tube, but squashing high-tension leads

RIGHT **On top of the cam cover on the left of the photograph can be seen the D-type plug lead separator.** *(Author)*

ABOVE Fitting the light alloy cooling system header tank. *(Author)*

ABOVE RIGHT The Lucas RCPR 11A lightweight aircraft-type battery was located under the bonnet behind the right-hand-side wheel arch. *(Author)*

together like that isn't very healthy and it can, by a process of induction, cause cross-firing. So it's better to keep the wires separate from each other. Also, if you're working on the car and have to take the plugs out quickly you can be absolutely sure you can put the leads back on the right plugs. So that was another good reason for it. It prevents cross-firing and makes maintenance easier.'

Talking about the cam covers (see photograph on page 79) Chris said: 'There are a lot of components which are things of beauty. Those are the special cam covers with the breathers on,

and the other thing about the D-type cam cover which isn't immediately obvious is there's no filler in it. Normally on a Jaguar one has a filler cap, but this doesn't because you don't put the oil in the engine because it's a dry sump engine, you put it in the tank.'

Cooling system

A separate light alloy header tank, located between the engine and radiator, allows the bonnet height to be kept low. Just like everything else on the D-type its almost aerofoil shape allows it to fit snugly beneath the bonnet

LEFT Two three-branch welded exhaust manifolds took the exhaust gases via two short flexible pipes to the two main outlet pipes. *(Author)*

BELOW Dry sump tank and exhausts as seen on a 3.8-litre engine. *(Author)*

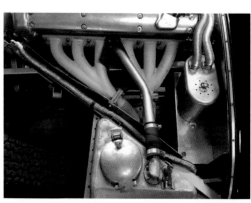

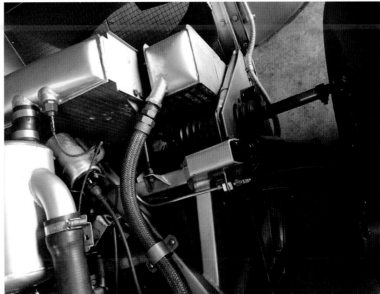

in what Chris Keith-Lucas describes as a 'beautifully aircrafty way'.

Transmission

Clutch

Power is transmitted via a triple-plate Borg & Beck clutch to a four-speed synchromesh gearbox.

The clutch is hydraulically operated through a master cylinder located on the pedal bracket and a slave cylinder located on the upper left-hand side of the clutch housing. The reservoir is integral with the master cylinder assembly and, for filling and topping-up purposes, is located in the compartment under the air duct.

The main clutch body contains three sets of internal splines, equally spaced around its bore, mating with the external splines on the two intermediate driving plates. The rear clutch-driven plate is attached to a centrepiece that's internally splined to mate with the gearbox input shaft and contains three sets of external splines, carrying the first and second driven plates.

The starter ring is bolted on to the centre

section of the clutch assembly. The engine doesn't have a flywheel, the effect instead being produced by the combined mass of the triple-plate clutch and the starter ring.

Gearbox

The cast iron main gearbox casing and aluminium cover of the D-type gearbox is essentially the same as that used on the C-type, but with completely redesigned internals. It was Jaguar's first all-synchromesh gearbox and featured single helical gears with special close

ratios. First gear is 2.144:1, second 1.645:1, third 1.280:1 and a direct fourth at 1:1. A splined layshaft with removable gears allows for easy change of individual gears.

An H-pattern gear change is used, with reverse on a sprung dogleg to the left and forward. Gears are selected by a short change lever placed just behind the gearbox unit. From the rear of the gearbox a Hardy Spicer propeller shaft links to the Salisbury rear axle with a final drive ratio of 3.54:1.

The gearbox also features an external

interlock system that was retrofitted to the D-type after it was discovered during early testing that it had a tendency to jump out of second gear. Fitted to the transmission, the mechanism runs from the arm at the top to the plate and operates a bellcrank located behind the gearstick. A pin goes down through this to the first- and second-gear selector shaft and prevents second gear being engaged or disengaged without the clutch being fully released. 'You can't get it in or out of gear unless you're sitting in the car with your foot on the clutch,' explained Chris Keith-Lucas. 'If you just lean in and try to get it out of first, it's completely locked.'

The aluminium rear cover of the gearbox encloses a small reciprocating oil pump that feeds directly to the gears through the hollow main shaft. The cover also provides the mounting for the Plessey pump for the brakes, which is driven by worm gears.

The starter motor is mounted on top of the gearbox and locates through a large opening on the top of the bellhousing from the back rather than the front. This is because the D-type doesn't have a conventional flywheel like other Jaguars. Instead, the clutch is bolted to an adaptor plate, the diameter of which is so small that the starter motor wouldn't engage with the teeth if it were mounted from the front. Locating it from the back allows closer access to the

centreline and hence to the teeth.

The Plessey brake hydraulic pump attaches to the side of the gearbox, and is driven via a splined shaft. A vertical milled groove running downwards from the bottom of the mounting hole prevents the gearbox from filling up with brake fluid in the event of the pump's seal failing. Instead the groove acts as a drain, allowing brake fluid to run out and indicate that there's a problem. On the other side of the gearbox a similar, but smaller and lighter, skew gear drives the speedometer.

ABOVE LEFT The pad on the side of the gearbox to which the Plessey pump attaches, with the splined internal gear just visible. Note the groove to allow brake fluid to drain in the event of a pump seal failure – see text. *(Author)*

ABOVE Gearbox installed inside cockpit. The Plessey pump has yet to be connected and the interlock fitted. *(Author)*

LEFT Traditional Jaguar competition gear lever knob. *(Author)*

RIGHT The rear axle of the D-type is extremely heavy. *(Author)*

BELOW A view of a complete D-type rear axle. *(Author)*

BELOW RIGHT The trailing arms of the rear suspension locate into the bracket at the end of the axle. *(Author)*

Rear axle

The Salisbury live rear axle incorporates a Powr-Lok limited slip differential and peg-drive centre-lock hubs. Later works cars had a ZF limited slip diff. The standard final drive ratio of the rear axle is 3.54:1, but the following alternative ratios were also available: 2.79:1; 2.93:1; 3.31:1; 3.92:1; 4.09:1; 4.27:1; and 4.55:1.

The rear axle is almost a standard Jaguar part. There was an attempt at the time to use production components in order to promote the sale of production cars, using the company's success in racing 'to improve the breed'.

RIGHT The axle is attached to the trailing arms of the rear suspension. *(Author)*

BELOW The 3.77 indicates the final drive ratio of this particular rear axle. *(Author)*

Cockpit and instruments

Windscreen

The cockpit of the D-type has a single wrap-around Perspex windscreen on the driver's side, with the passenger seat covered by a quick-release metal tonneau. From 1956 onwards the regulations called for a full-width screen. Jaguar also fitted a Vybak clear plastic tonneau to reduce wind resistance.

Initially the car had a single driver's door, made from 18swg. In the earlier cars this was 18.5in long but it was increased to 19.7in and a passenger door fitted in order to comply with the Appendix C regulations that came into force for 1957.

Dashboard and instruments

The original 1954 cars had a curved dashboard offset to the left of the driver but this was replaced on subsequent models with a standard straight dash. All of the instruments fall easily to hand and the dashboard on standard production cars comprises a speedometer reading up to 180mph, an 8,000rpm chronometric tachometer, red-lined at 5,750rpm with telltale needle to record maximum revs; and oil pressure and water temperature gauges. The speedometer was omitted in later works cars. There was no fuel gauge, as the bag

TOP Jaguar test driver Les Botterill tests XKD 602 fitted with a full-width screen at Lindley in May 1956.
(John Pearson collection)

ABOVE This photograph of XKD 602 at Browns Lane clearly shows the Vybak plastic tonneau over the passenger seat.
(John Pearson collection)

LEFT D-types at the 2015 Goodwood Revival, showing the single wrap-around windscreen of the pre-1956 models. *(Author)*

ABOVE Curved dashboard as fitted to original 1954 D-types. *(Author)*

ABOVE RIGHT The steering wheel was 15in in diameter, with two full turns lock-to-lock. *(Author)*

RIGHT Cockpit of production D-type showing dashboard with instruments easily to hand. *(Author)*

RIGHT The 8,000rpm tachometer included a telltale needle to record maximum revs and was red-lined at 5,750rpm. *(Author)*

FAR RIGHT Oil pressure and water temperature gauges. *(Author)*

ABOVE The fuse boxes and Lucas RB310 voltage regulator were located on the left-hand side of the dashboard and left uncovered to provide easy access. *(Author)*

LEFT The light switches for dashboard (panel), sidelights, headlights, main beam and dipped beam are located on the left side of the dashboard, along with the Bakelite manual contact starter switch. *(Author)*

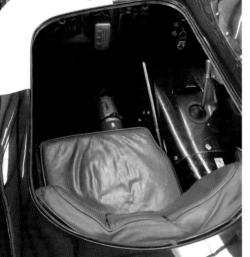

FAR LEFT With the passenger-side tonneau cover removed, the passenger seat, handbrake and gearstick can be clearly seen. *(Author)*

LEFT The headrest fairing and the tail fin were combined as a single unit. The seat backs and squabs were made to be quickly detachable to accommodate different drivers. All of the upholstery was Dunlopillow. *(Author)*

FAR LEFT The interior of the D-type was finished either matt black or in the same colour as the body. *(Author)*

LEFT The steering wheel locates on the splines on the steering column, adjustable for height at the top bearing. *(Author)*

tank didn't have provision for a sender unit. 'You'd just open the filler flap and have a look,' explained Chris Keith-Lucas.

Le Mans regulations dictated that only tools carried on the car could be used to work on it away from the pits, so items such as a jack, hammer and tool-roll were carried in a toolbox hole located underneath the passenger seat.

Ancillaries

Radiator and oil cooler

Both the oil and coolant radiators were made of light alloy by Marston Excelsior. The radiator system on the works cars pressurised to 4psi by means of an ERF valve unit in the back of the tank, whereas production cars had a standard pressure cap. The modern radiators faithfully reproduce the original design.

The water header tank is located behind the radiator. A tag on the top of the tank is fitted for attachment of a lock wire. Le Mans regulations from 1954 onwards stipulated a minimum distance of 30 laps (up from the previous 28) between replenishments of fuel, oil and water, so seals were placed by *plombeurs* on the filler caps of each car prior to the start of the race and again each time the oil or water was topped up.

Water pump

The water pump is of conventional design but with an efficient impeller and cast aluminium casing in order to save weight. The pulley is made of two parts, with the front and rear sections joined by means of a fine thread that facilitates tightening. Rotating one in relation to the other increases or decreases the width of the vee for the drive belt, thereby adjusting the tension of the belt, much like the automatic transmission system used by DAF many years later. 'You just push the two cones together and the effective diameter increases,' explained Chris. 'It's rather a nice touch and a real quality touch. That's for the drive belt that goes from the crank to the water pump. The pulley to the

OPPOSITE The water header tank is located behind the radiator. Note the tag on the top for attachment of a lock wire. (Author)

TOP The water radiator being fitted into position. (Author)

ABOVE The modern radiators faithfully reproduce the original design. (Author)

LEFT The water pump in position on the front of the cylinder block. (Author)

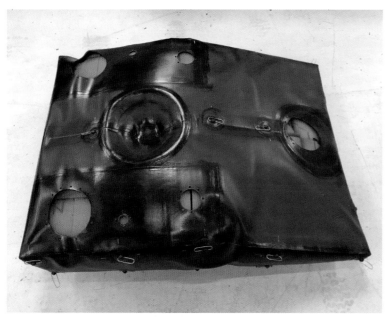

ABOVE **The deformable-bag fuel tank.** *(Author)*

dynamo is adjusted in a conventional way – you just rock the dynamo away to tighten it up.'

He also believes that the system is unique to the D-type. 'I haven't seen it on any other Jaguar,' he said. 'It may be on some other cars, but it was the only time Jaguar used it. And it's very neat and tidy. But for a production car it would probably be too complicated and expensive.'

Coolant circulates from the cylinder head and block via the inlet manifold to an aluminium header tank. Internal baffles ensure an equal flow from the two outlets into either side of the Marston aircraft-type radiator. Like the C-type, the D-type doesn't incorporate a cooling fan.

Fuel tanks and pumps

The fuel is contained within a deformable bag tank in the tail of the car, although in the early

LEFT **The circular studded hoops on top of the workbench are the nut rings, or stud rings as they're sometimes called. These hold the flexible fuel tank to the fuel tank cell and secure the cover plates to the bodywork.** *(Author)*

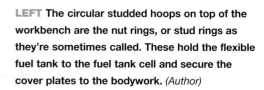

BELOW LEFT **The fuel pumps were attached to the rear bulkhead, one on each side.** *(Author)*

BELOW **Close-up of fuel pump with non-standard flexible hose.** *(Author)*

models two separate tanks were used. Twin petrol pumps, located behind the rear bulkhead, connected these via a common delivery pipe to the carburettors. All the fuel lines are Dunlop aircraft fittings.

Specialist tools

The following specialised service tools were listed as being available from the factory:

Cradle and slings for removing engine	PL 3493
Rear hub arresting spanner	TFG 666
Rear hub extractor	TFG 667
Tie-rod inner ball joint 'C' spanner	TFG 668
Tie-rod inner ball joint hexagon spanner	TFG 669
Rear hub nut spanner	TFG 670
Spanner for rear torsion bar locknut	TFG 671
Front and rear suspension setting bars	TFG 672
Front and rear suspension setting bar pins	TFG 673
Axle shaft extractor	TFG 697

Lighting

All lighting on the D-type was provided by Lucas. The headlamps are 12V 45/40W Lucas Le Mans 24- Hour headlamps, with the name written in the glass. Sidelights are 6W, tail and stop lights 6/21W and the competition number illumination light also 6W. Panel lights are 2.2W.

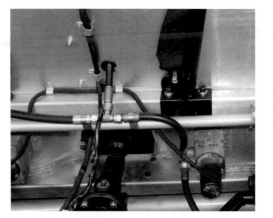

LEFT The feeds from the left- and right-hand fuel pumps meet in the middle and go forward as a single pipe towards the front of the car. *(CKL)*

LEFT The fuel filler cap is located directly behind the driver's head. *(Author)*

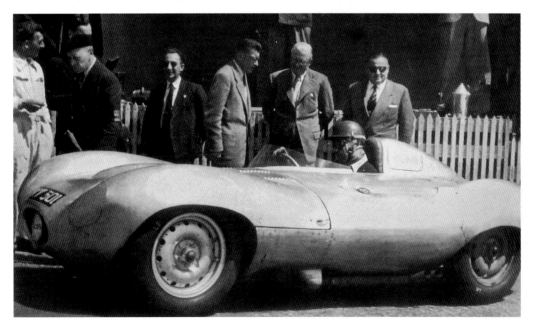

LEFT XKC 401 with its single, centrally mounted spotlight pictured at the Le Mans trials in 1954. Sitting in the car is Tony Rolt while standing behind it are Bill Heynes (far right) and, next to him, William Lyons.

(John Pearson collection)

RIGHT XKC 401
pictured at the Lindley
test track with the
previously centrally
mounted spotlight now
moved to the nearside
of the nose, adjacent
to the headlamp.
(JDHT)

The first prototype D-type, XKC 401, sported a single, centrally mounted spotlight in the elliptical opening in the nose of the car, but by the time the cars arrived at Le Mans in 1954 for their competition debut this had been moved to the nearside, between the existing headlamp and the opening. In 1955 this third lamp was removed completely and the two headlamps uprated to 100W.

'Things like the tail lights were out of the standard British parts bin,' explained Chris Keith-Lucas, 'and you'll find those same lights, or versions of them, on Morris Minors, Triumphs and MGs. In fact the tail light is absolutely identical to that of the MGA, because it uses the same bezel. Mostly they have the same lens but there were a great assortment of different bezels.'

Supplementary brake lights were fitted because, at Le Mans, drivers could be flagged in by the officials if they weren't working properly.

BELOW Original
headlamps from a
D-type, with 'Le Mans'
and '24' inscribed on
them. *(Author)*

ABOVE Tail and stop lights were from the standard British 'parts bin'. *(Author)*

RIGHT Wiring diagram for the D-type taken from 'Servicing Details for XK120 D Type' handbook. *(John Pearson collection)*

Wheels

The D-type featured 16in Dunlop pressed alloy disc, centre-lock wheels, as opposed to the spoked wheels of the C-type, but retained the five-inch rim. These were stronger, lighter (15lb as opposed to 18lb) and easier to change. Tyres were 6.50-16in Dunlop racing tyres.

BELOW Archetypical Dunlop wheel with three-eared spinner. The Dunlop stickers were fitted at 90° to the valve. *(Author)*

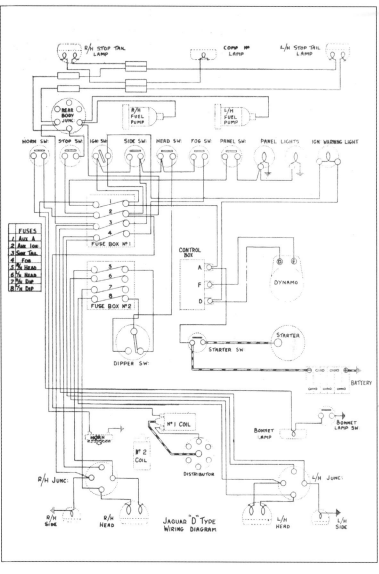

LEFT Without the central dust cap fitted, the adjusting nut for the hub bearing is visible. *(Author)*

BELOW The spare wheel is located inside the boot. *(CKL)*

The finished article

RIGHT The engine has yet to be installed but the rolling chassis with suspension and wheels attached is complete. *(Author)*

BELOW As mentioned in an earlier caption, the small roll hoop is a modern preference for some owners and drivers for competition use. *(Author)*

ABOVE Even without its engine or front and rear bodywork, the car is unmistakably a **D-type**. *(Author)*

LEFT The rolling chassis is complete and ready to have the engine installed. *(Author)*

BELOW The engine is installed. Only the exhaust manifolds are still to be fitted. *(Author)*

LEFT The oil catch-tank sitting above the passenger footbox is a modern FIA requirement. In period the oil tank just vented straight down and on to the track. *(Author)*

BELOW The completed car, fully restored, sits resplendent in the sunshine outside CKL's premises. *(CKL)*

Chapter Three

The engineer's view

The D-type incorporated a number of totally revolutionary ideas, drawing heavily on the aviation industry for its design, both in appearance and construction. Its oval-section monocoque helped reduce frontal area while still increasing torsional stiffness, and it was the first production car to use disc brakes. It's a design which still fascinates and impresses engineers today.

OPPOSITE Beneath the bonnet of the D-type, all the components are shaped and arranged to match the external aerodynamic shape. *(LAT)*

Chris Keith-Lucas – CKL Developments

Chris Keith-Lucas reckons that he's had contact with a large proportion of all the D-types that have ever existed over the last 40-plus years, even if it was only to supply a new rear light cover, and has had contact with many of the owners as well. He's accepted as a world expert on the cars and is often called upon to give his opinion on the provenance of Jaguars and D-types in particular.

'The whole thing about a D-type is that it contained lots of really, really revolutionary ideas at the time,' he explained. 'Now it's a thing that we look back on and think "what a pretty car", but at the time it was totally cutting-edge and miles ahead of the fairly homespun designs that were sports racing cars of the period. It was designed entirely with one thing in mind, which was to win Le Mans.

'The master stroke was bringing an aircraft man, Malcolm Sayer, in to guide the design, because not only was it therefore technically right up to date, because the aircraft industry was well ahead of the car industry at that time

thanks to there having just been a rather large war, but it brought a whole lot of new practices into construction and new concepts, so the whole car was bristling with aircraft reference to various things.'

Up to this point it hadn't been widely recognised that aircraft technology could be transferred to cars, but, as Chris explained, this was the time at which it actually happened. 'If you look at the way an aircraft engine of that time was held into its fuselage or a wing,' he said, 'it was an aluminium structure with a bulkhead and then tubular, triangulated frames which held the engine to that. And then you look at a D-type, and what have you got? You've got the engine nacelle with a triangulated, tubular frame holding a heavy lump of an engine to it in the most minimalistic way. And, for the first time, they managed to get rid of the whole concept of having a chassis to which the engine and body were bolted and the entire thing became one whole design.

'The C-type had been revolutionary because it was the world's first sports racing car spaceframe chassis, made of steel tubes, but even though that design was only a couple of

BELOW Malcolm Sayer's design drawing for the long-nose D-type.
(Philip Porter collection)

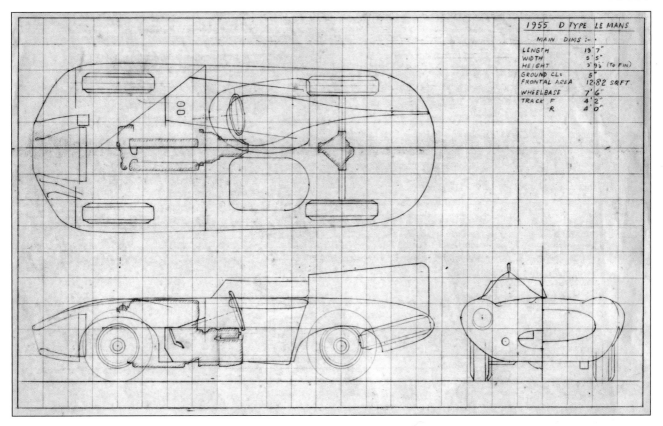

ABOVE **The long-nose D-type prototype undergoing testing.** (Philip Porter collection)

years old Malcolm Sayer actually abandoned it and leapt straight to the monocoque aluminium structure with the tubular frames. And also, cunningly, the suspension is bolted to more or less same bits of the chassis frame – the tubular front subframe – that the engine is. So the loads from the engine can go straight into the suspension without having to pass through some gigantic steel ladder chassis that other cars had. So it was really a work of genius.

'He had to use production axles, production engines and gearboxes, or something very, very like them,' he continued, 'because part of what Jaguar was trying to achieve was that, although this thing could win Le Mans, it was essentially the same as the car that you were going to drive to the office in.

'So if you're an engineer, it's absolutely fascinating to see how they did that and what a huge leap in thinking it was at the time. And when you open the bonnet on a D-type, you can really see how the thinking extended right through the car in a sort of holistic way. You lift the bonnet of a D-type and immediately it's an imprint of everything that's underneath it. The dry sump tank is shaped exactly to the skin, the engine is tilted over and it just goes in the little bump on the bonnet, the airbox just fits under the skin. Even the associated oil tanks, radiators, oil coolers and carburettors fit the aerodynamic shape that's on the outside. Lift it up and the shape's still there.

'The whole thing is designed as one, whereas with something like a Cooper or a Lister, although they produced a more successful road-holding car, somebody would have been asked to design a nice, swoopy shape, and then they'd have had the skin made and then they'd stick an engine in the chassis, drop the body over and think "Where can we put this?" and "Where can we put that?" But Sayer's design was just hugely clever. Even things like the carburettor airboxes were shaped aerodynamically with the skin – it's totally different. The D-type was absolutely designed as one nugget of quality, so I think it's massively important.

'I don't think people quite understand that when they see it, because they don't perhaps

Due to their proximity of the engine and suspension mountings on the chassis frame, loads from the engine can be transferred directly into the suspension without having to pass through a long chassis. *(LAT)*

have quite the sense of racing history and what other cars were like around that time. But the D-type was just very, very advanced, and you want to have a look at one, as I say, with an airbox on, with the oil tanks and everything else in position, and you suddenly realise that's what they're shaped from. Even the wheels, that slight rise over the wheels – everything just fits in that shape perfectly.

'Compare it to an XK120 with a pressed steel chassis frame – let's screw a tank here and an engine there and a gearbox there, oh and we've got to stick some wheels on it. Absolutely pre-war. It could have been an early 1930s car almost, although it had good performance. They hadn't started thinking technically again at that time. And then you progress to the C-type, where there's some really revolutionary ideas of using the same mechanical bits in a much cleverer-constructed body with a spaceframe chassis and so forth. And then to have the courage to completely ditch that, which was completely revolutionary then, and go straight to the monocoque within two years of coming up with the tubular spaceframe – that was really brave.

'To start off with, the subframe was made of alloy tubes welded to the alloy monocoque, which was great but they hadn't really thought about what happens when it crashes, which is that it was really difficult to repair. The great thing with the steel one is you can unbolt the subframe and bolt a new one in. And of course, that continued through the E-type with that thinking extended even to breaking the subframe down into bits so you could put in a new left, or a new right, or a new middle, so they made it in smaller chunks to make it even more easy to repair.

'One of the most interesting things is the fact that they had an oval section, because they went with a monocoque, using aeroplane thinking – they were able to go to an oval section rather than square section, which reduced the frontal area and increased the torsional stiffness. It was also the car with the first production disc brake, and that, of course, is something that that car has given to the whole of the rest of the motoring world. This was the car that did it. They did try them out on the C-type – a couple of prototype brake systems on that were disc – but the D-type was designed to have disc brakes from scratch.

'It's the most fascinating system because in some ways it was really, really clever in that they realised at the outset that it was going to get extremely hot, so they found a way of moving the piston blocks well away from the source of heat, so that you could run it with ordinary brake fluid and it would never boil. Nowadays we're running race fluid and vented discs and things like that, but the D-type's disc brakes could stop the car from 200mph on the Mulsanne Straight, glowing red hot, and not lose the pedal. And the pads were something like an inch and a quarter thick when they were new, so that in a 24-hour race you'd never have to put in new pads. Which is just as well, because it's a day's job to put them in!

'The brake system is one that you can have a lot of fun with, but it also had some serious shortcomings. The thinking again came from the aircraft industry. They felt that they needed external assistance to provide the pressure that a disc brake would need to push the pads on. So they thought, well, aircraft have hydraulic systems to work control surfaces and so forth, so this will have to have a hydraulic system. Where are we going to drive the pump from? Well the engine revs are going up and down all the time, unlike in an aircraft engine, so you can't use the engine, but the wheels are going round all the time, so any time that you need hydraulic pressure the wheels are rotating, so let's run it off the back of the transmission.

'That was a great idea, but the thing is, when the car's going very slowly, there's very little hydraulic pressure, and when it's approaching 200mph there's a hell of a lot of hydraulic pressure. So you've got this variable pressure, which means that at walking speed you stand on the brakes and virtually nothing happens and when you come really fast on the fastest straight on the circuit, and you leave your braking to the last possible minute, when you hit the brakes they're so effective that they lock up, and the rears lock first; and when the rear brakes lock the transmission no longer goes round and the pump is no longer pumping and suddenly there are no brakes at all. Which, if you could've harnessed that effect, you could almost have come up with the world's first ABS. It wasn't quite done, and there were some

big accidents in exactly those circumstances until they really understood things better. But the D-type was the world's first production disc-brake car, and now disc brakes are in everything we drive and we don't give them a second thought. The D-type was the car that brought that in, as well as the monocoque.

'To me the appeal is totally that it's an absolutely revolutionary car. I'm very interested in the history of design, and if you look at the pace at which mechanical design progressed between 1950 and 1970 you'll see that it's really slowed up since. In electronics and other things it's gone ahead, but to go from something like an XK120 in 1950 to what sports car racing became 20 years later, it was just a huge leap. The C-type represented the first leap because it was the first sports racing car to have a tubular spaceframe chassis, and within only two years Jaguars had jumped that idea and gone on to monocoque. And nobody else was looking at monocoques for race cars, I don't think. But to make that jump and to bring people in from the aircraft industry to do it, who brought totally revolutionary ideas with them, not only in the design of the body but in the whole concept of working towards reliability through quality, and bringing in the aircraft technology which provided that reliability. If you look at the fuel systems that were on the C-types they were an absolute old lash-up in comparison, whereas

BELOW **The D-type featured the first production disc brake, developed by Dunlop.** *(LAT)*

in a D-type it was all aircraft fittings – aircraft pipes, aircraft bag tank, all that. It also had amazingly low drag for the period and was amazingly effective.'

Gary Pearson – Pearsons Engineering

'There are very few bad bits on a D-type really. It was designed to do a job, which it did fantastically well, which was to win Le Mans. Because it's so well packaged, and everything is so neatly packaged, it means some of the servicing isn't as straightforward as it is on most Jaguars. So to service the clutch you've got to take the engine and the gearbox out, things like that, but it's not the end of the world.

'The brakes were fantastic in period but they're complex and they take quite a lot of servicing. The pistons run on a flat washer seal, and as soon as they wear a little bit they're prone to leak, particularly after use when they've cooled down. You come to the car the next day and you find you've got brake fluid leaking. Servicing the brakes isn't a quick job. It

takes between a day and two days to reseal all the pistons. To change the pads you've got to completely strip the brake calipers down, and the pads are bonded to the back plate, so it's a two-day job to change the brake pads on a car. But they were the best in the world. They were the reason that the cars won Le Mans. So to do 24 hours on just one set of brakes, they did the job they were designed for, didn't they?

'The car has a very heavy live rear axle, which wasn't great for racing on circuits other than Le Mans. They weren't good on the Mille Miglia or the Nürburgring, which were bumpy road circuits. But apart from that, all the features are outstanding. I think for a 1954 car to have this monocoque design, disc brakes and rubber fuel cell, it was all so far ahead of its time.

'What made the D-type so special? For me, it was a car I was brought up with, so I've always been interested in them. But as an engineer it comes back to the aircraft stuff. The concept and the engineering in these cars was really cutting-edge stuff. Ferraris had a magnificent engine and that was about it, and a tractor of a car. What Jaguar did was

RIGHT This view of the front brake assembly on XKD 603 shows the more conventional caliper with 'quick change' pads as fitted to the 1956 works cars.
(John Pearson collection)

just fantastic engineering with a much smaller engine. It was just brilliant foresight by the people at Jaguar in the early 1950s when they decided they wanted to go motor racing and how quickly they moved from the XK120 to the C-type, to the lightweight C-type. And to go from that to the D-type in another year is absolutely staggering – the ambition, and what they achieved.'

John Pearson – Pearsons Engineering

'**M**any people were brought in from the armed forces or from industries involved in the war, that's the secret – blokes who knew what they were doing and had a lot of aircraft experience. But really, when you look at the frame of a D-type, the chassis – most people think it ends at the front of the monocoque, but it goes right through the car and it really could easily have been the bearer for an aircraft engine, because the engine would slot into it. And the fact that it had a cross-member at the front you could put the suspension on meant you could build a car round it.

'The Dunlop calipers on the brakes were developed from the aviation industry. Aeroplanes had these types of brakes before cars did. And Jaguar and Dunlop pioneered a partnership in this country, developing the disc brake over the drum brake. The last series of cars – the '56 cars – had what we'd now recognise as a more conventional caliper with just two pads, two pistons, one each side, instead of six, because it meant you could just pull the pads out and put new ones in; but on the older ones you have to dismantle the whole thing, which is very time-consuming. But at the '55 Le Mans the cars had actually run down to the backing plates of the pads, so they knew they were in trouble on long races.'

Dick Crosthwaite – Crosthwaite and Gardiner

'**S**ome cars are so good that you can tell as soon as you get in and you've done 100 yards down the road, and you think "Bloody hell, this is a good thing"; and there

ABOVE The rear brake assembly on XKD 603 showing the caliper and handbrake mechanism.
(John Pearson collection)

are others that are dogs. And D-types, they just drive so well and they're easy to drive.

'Just ask anyone who's driven one. They're probably even better on the road than on the track. It's like riding a motorbike – if you want to pass a car in front you just kind of lean to the right and you've passed about four cars before you know it.

'It's only standard Jaguar stuff really, nothing very clever about the bits. The gearbox was quite complicated. It was a special gearbox only because they wanted a very high first for Mulsanne Corner at the end of the straight at Le Mans, and that necessitated a bit of a redesign of the gearbox, so everything in the gearbox is special. The synchromesh is quite complicated but there's nothing you can't fix.

'It's just a Jaguar engine with a dry sump kit on it. It's a bit of a pig to get in and out, and if you want the gearbox out you're in trouble. To get the engine out you've either got to take the front off the frames and pull the engine out frontwards, or you've got to take the cylinder head off and drop it down. It's not the easiest thing to get out but, as I say, most of it is pretty standard sort of stuff. It was all sourced from the parts bins. All the front suspension is special in that the wishbones are a different length and things, but all the ball joints and other bits are just standard road car stuff. Brilliant things. You don't really need to do much. The engine will go for two or three years without touching it.'

Chapter Four

The driver's view

With its live rear axle, the D-type was more at home on circuits like Le Mans, for which it was designed, than more sinuous and bumpy tracks such as the Nürburgring but, nevertheless, it has been described as the ultimate road/race car. In this chapter, nine drivers, both period and modern, describe their experiences and impressions behind the wheel.

OPPOSITE Mike Hawthorn driving XKD 506, which he shared with Desmond Titterington, at the 1955 Tourist Trophy at Dundrod. The pair led much of the race but retired when the engine seized, only two laps from the finish. *(LAT)*

Ron Flockhart

Ecurie Ecosse driver and Le Mans winner 1956 and 1957

In a letter from Ron Flockhart to Lord Montagu of Beaulieu, written in 1961, Flockhart described his impressions of driving a D-type Jaguar, in particular along the Mulsanne Straight at Le Mans.

'One impression I have of the "D" type Jaguar which is probably unique, is that its handling characteristics are similar to that of the "D" type ERA.

'I found at Le Mans particularly with the tail fin, that the faster it went the more stable the car became. It was my practice to relax completely down the Mulsanne straight (race traffic permitting!) and flex my fingers and arms, the car steering itself at around 170mph. A good personal test of "Chicken or Hero Driver", was to take the slight right hand kink at the end of the Mulsanne straight absolutely flat – no secret cheating by easing off a couple of hundred rpm but an honest

5,800 rpm on the 1957 3.8 litre – It could be done, but only just. If the track were damp, then this game was for Chicken Drivers only. Both Ivor Bueb and I discovered this in our own fashion – something the spectators missed! However in conditions of crosswind this was not possible and I recall once at Goodwood one blustery day at practice where the Jaguar with tail fin was a handful through Fordwater and past the pits.'

He added: 'The 3.4 litre Jaguar engine (and the later 3.8 litre) in my opinion come under the same category as the Gypsy Major and Rolls Royce Merlin aero engines, it feels as if it would go on for ever. However, the 3 litre version was never as successful, I don't think the design lent itself to continued operation above 6,000 rpm. There was no marked difference in performance between the Lucas fuel injection 3.8 litre Jaguar and the normal Weber carburettor "D" type. The only noticeable difference being that the Lucas injection gave smoother acceleration with no spitting back and hesitation round a slow corner on part throttle.'

BELOW

Ron Flockhart at the wheel of XKD 501 leads Ecurie Ecosse team-mate Desmond Titterington in XKD 502 at the 1956 Whit Monday meeting at Goodwood. The pair finished second and third behind the D-type of Bob Berry. *(LAT)*

Peter Sutcliffe

Owned and raced XKD 504 in 1961–63

'I just found it was the most marvellous car to drive – wonderfully controllable. I used to drive the D-type to events around Yorkshire, just drive it on the road to Rufforth or wherever I happened to be racing it, but mostly it went on the trailer unless I was just driving it on the road for fun. And it is a wonderful road car. Tractable, easy to drive, no tricks to it. It was a lovely gentle car to drive on the road if that's the mood that you were in; lovely supple suspension.

'And in those pre-motorway days, the ability to effortlessly overtake traffic and cover distance with ease and with great margins of safety was a wonderful experience, and very useful training for the track too. There was none of the headlight flashing, hooting and rude waving that one receives nowadays if one attempts to get along on our ordinary roads. In those days there wasn't much to challenge a D-type on the road! There was no need for a horn, as traffic seemed to instinctively "step aside" if and when they caught sight of you in their mirror.

'It was quite easy to drive at night, I loved it. The instrument lights were entirely adequate to see what was going on inside the car. And everything in the car was absolutely subconsciously to hand anyway, because of the way it was designed. Everything was exactly where you would be glad to find it. Any race over an hour or more I'd really look forward to because that's when I really got into the swing of things.'

Chris Keith-Lucas

Director CKL Developments

'They're like a four-wheeled motorbike; and the performance – was it 0–60 in about five seconds? Now think of that in a world where everybody was pottering around in a Morris Minor or an Austin A30 or whatever, and something of that performance is also on the road. Even now, they're really adrenaline-inducing cars. On the road you come up behind something and you're in front of it before you can blink. Just great fun. So a very "alive" car, and because the seat is part of the monocoque the whole feel of the car is transmitted through to you. We've found that if you put a racing seat into an old '50s sports car, drivers immediately go faster because they can feel the car underneath them, feel what it's doing. But the D-type gives you that anyway because you're part of the car, you're part of the machine. So you sit in it, part of it, not on it. So it's a great driving experience. A D-type really is a living thing. You have to drive it to find out.'

Paul Frère

Jaguar works driver

In his autobiography, *Starting Grid to Chequered Flag*, Frère described some of the shortcomings of the D-type on twisty and bumpy tracks such as the Nürburgring, where he crashed XKD 603 in practice for the 1956 Nürburgring 1,000km.

'The Jaguars, with their solid and unsprung rear axle, were not at all suited to the bumpy

ABOVE
On lap three of the 1956 Le Mans 24 Hours, Paul Frère spun his works D-type (No.2 – XKD 603) in the Esses and hit the wall hard. His teammate Jack Fairman (No.3 – XKD 602) spun in avoidance, but was himself hit by the works Ferrari 625 LM (No.11) of Alfonso de Portago. All three cars subsequently retired as a consequence.
(LAT)

Nürburgring course. In many places our speed was limited not so much by the convolutions of the circuit as by our desire to keep the car in one piece. Along the whole stretch leading from Breitscheid to Karussell the back wheels were more in the air than on the ground, and with a full tank the suspension was bottoming frequently.'

Gary Pearson

Pearsons Engineering

Gary Pearson has driven both the older aluminium-framed D-types and the later steel-framed versions, and finds the former a lot more rigid. 'I was lucky enough to race in the car several times and it's one of the nicest chassis that I've driven. It's really taut.' Pearson attributes this to the chassis, or frame, being integral to the whole structure: 'The front frame goes all the way through, welded to the rear subframe and welded to the body – it's all one,' he explained. 'It's more rigid.'

'The performance? Bear in mind they weigh about a ton – a production spec D-type produces about 160–170bhp per ton. For a mid-1950s car it's exciting performance even now.'

The smile on Pearson's face as he enthuses about the D-type says it all. 'Best car in the world,' he said. 'I've been lucky. I've driven not just Jaguars but a lot of nice cars, and I've raced a lot of nice cars as well, but I really think the D-type is one of the best cars in the world. Not just the concept, but the way they perform and feel. Certain cars you know are

proper long-distance cars. They're designed to be driven comfortably for a long period of time. You sit in the car, you're comfortable. Everything is where it should be, you don't feel tired, you don't get buffeted. The D-type is like that, a Porsche 956 is like that and an XJR12 Jaguar is like that. A GT40, on the other hand, isn't that comfortable to drive or to race. You sit in it and everything is designed to be where it needs to be, but the D-type is probably the best of all.'

John Pearson

Pearsons Engineering

'There's only one thing that's critical – and it's so difficult to get this into newcomers – which is that you mustn't slip the clutch. If you took one up to the service department, Lofty England used to stand there with his famous forefinger up; he'd come down and see me off. "Now, Mr Pearson," – everyone was mister so-and-so – "don't forget – tickover!" God help you if you didn't. You were supposed to take them off on tickover. "Do not slip that clutch!" Tickover was 700 revs. What you must never do is drive it on to the back of a lorry or drive it on to a trailer, you must never do that. Most people who do that bugger the clutch in no time.'

Win Percy

Driven various D-types at many historic meetings

'I first drove a D-type at Silverstone one year at the Coys Festival, as it was then. Valentine Lindsay was out in his father's road-going "D", and for some reason he wasn't happy with it and asked me to try it. So I went out and did a lap, came in and said, "Well, I don't really know what to say mate, there's no brakes." So he said, "No, Win, that's what they're like. What you mustn't do is lock the back axle because, if you do, the pump to the rear brakes doesn't work and all you've got is the front brakes."

'So I went back out and I drove it and I loved it. I just loved the drifting side of it, trying to keep your rolling speed up without braking too much, a bit like NASCAR, where you try not to over-brake into the banking. You keep your

BELOW John Pearson at the wheel of his D-type XKD 543.
(Author)

rolling speed up all the time, just braking gently to kill off the speed you don't want.

'So he asked me if I'd like to race it the next day and I did. I remember I overtook Steve O'Rourke coming down into Woodcote, and he came over afterwards when I was talking to Valentine and said, "Oh, that explains it!" I asked him what he meant and he said, "Well, I saw Valentine's car behind me, next minute there was a whoosh and it was in front of me, and I thought 'Oh my god, Valentine's on steroids today.'" And he was laughing away. He said, "Oh, I'm happy now. I couldn't work out what had happened."

'Then I went back one day to Silverstone practice day for something and Valentine was there again and so was Frank Sytner with the race-prepared JCB D-type. I'd been out in Valentine's car and done some times, and out

of interest Frank said "Do you want a go?" So I went out and did a few laps and I didn't enjoy it. Trying really hard I was only 0.2sec faster in that immensely prepared racing "D" than I was in Valentine's road car, and I couldn't work that out.'

At the inaugural Goodwood Revival in 1998 Win was again driving Valentine Lindsay's D-type. 'It was when Martin Brundle was in the yellow Belgian car [*Equipe Nationale Belge*], Stirling Moss was in the Aston DBR1 and they were dicing. And do you know, this road-going "D" went by the pair of them, and I was so chuffed with it. All of a sudden the cabin filled up with oil smoke, and the difference between a works drive and a private drive is that if something goes wrong you respect their money, their car, and you stop. With a works car it doesn't really matter what's

ABOVE Win Percy leading away in Nigel Webb's D-type, XKD 505, at the 2004 Le Mans Classic.
(Nigel Webb collection)

happening, if it's got four wheels and it's still running – you've got to risk your neck and keep going. Like at Le Mans; you have to do that – it's what you're paid to do. I came into the pit and unbelievably it was the breather pipe that had blown out of the gearbox. That's all it was, but I didn't know that.

'Again, it reinstated in my mind that you don't try to make that much of a race car of a D-type by stiffening it and doing other things to it. It's something odd about a "D" that you don't do that to necessarily get the best out of it.'

Win was then asked by Penny Griffiths-Woodley if he'd like to drive her D-type, which Don Law prepared and ran for the 1999 season. 'Her one request was that we didn't damage it, because she didn't want any paint on it, she wanted it original,' he explained.

'Well, it went well and I loved it, but the pop rivets creaked and when it was rainy you could see the rivulets of water running out of the holes and all sorts of things, and feel it flexing when you cornered it. So I had a wonderful time in that, came second to Peter Hardman in the Aston at the Goodwood Revival and had a ball in it.' A report of the event stated: 'Percy was driving Penny Griffiths-Woodley's amazingly original and unspoiled off-white car. Hardman was spectacular but Percy even more so. He took second place from Ian Donaldson's D-type as they passed a backmarker on either side going past the pits and into Madgwick.'

But the D-type which Win is most associated with is Nigel Webb's beautiful evocation of the 1955 Le Mans-winning car, XKD 505, which was prepared by Gary Pearson and immortalised in the DVD of him driving it around Goodwood, entitled *Sideways in a D-Type*.

'We did the first-ever Classic Le Mans in 2002 and won all four races, and one of the most memorable things was that a guy came up to me – a Frenchman – and he hugged me and he had tears in his eyes. He'd watched Le Mans every year since he was a boy, and he came to watch the Classic Le Mans and he said, "It was just like Hawthorn, Mr Percy. You've made my day. It was just amazing." He was hugging me and I thought, "Golly, are you all right?" He was really nice.'

Later that year Win drove Webb's D-type to second place in the Lavant Cup at the Goodwood Revival behind the Ferrari of Tony Dron. A contemporary report stated: 'Percy thrilled the Madgwick, St Mary's and Lavant crowds with huge tail-out slides in the Nigel Webb-entered D-type.'

'When we raced at Goodwood, we got second there with it, and Stirling Moss said to me, "Win, I've only ever seen people drive these properly a couple of times, and that was Mike [Hawthorn] and you." He said, "You've got it, whatever it is about a 'D', you've got it." And I really respect Stirling, so I felt really chuffed.'

The comparison with Hawthorn was also true when it came to the only major problem he had with the car. 'We were running third at Silverstone one year and a half-shaft broke,' he said. 'Apparently the only other guy that's ever broken a half-shaft was Hawthorn.' So was that down to the sideways driving style? 'I think so, yeah. Drifting, the half-shaft didn't like it. So they then checked it after that and lifed them, whereas we hadn't lifed that one at all. That was the only breakage we ever had. We never damaged the car, and we never had any mechanical problems, we never had to rebuild the engine or anything.

'The only other problem we had was when we took it to Australia for the Grand Prix support parade and the Philip Island Historic Meeting, and apart from one fuel pump which was playing up we'd have won both races. As it was we got two seconds because it didn't have the straight-line speed that I wanted, but I enjoyed it. It was damp as well – it was sideways.

'I must be honest, it's very physical, the "D", because you're straining to keep your back upright – not a very good seating position. It's not the most comfortable way of driving a motor car, to be honest. You've got no wrap-around seats like modern cars. You're sideways all the time, with your body trying to crawl out the car, especially if it's a right-hander.'

Win attributes his affinity with the D-type to an unlikely source. 'I remember my 1650 twin-cam Ford Anglia that I used to autocross, and I can only say that's where I got the ability to drive the "D",' he explained. 'That was with 5½in knobblies on the back, 3½in knobblies on the front, and a car with all the power in the world. No brakes on grass, drifting it in rallycross and autocross. And I honestly think that's where, if you call it skill, whatever you want to call it – that's where that ability came from. And I told Nigel that. I said, "I'm not being rude, but it's just like driving my Anglia. Too much power and no brakes, and you just drift it to keep your rolling speed up."

'It was amazing what we could do with the car. We had outright wins as well, and it was all about keeping your rolling speed up. If you over-braked and then thought you were going to power out of a corner, you couldn't, because you'd lose all your grip in the world. At Goodwood, the first time through Fordwater you could just do it flat the first lap but after that the tyres would lose their special bite and you had to feather them. Although I had a hell of a lead in the race at Goodwood the year I drove it there, I had to give way to Tony Dron in the end because he could just go through Fordwater flat and I couldn't.'

But it was running at the Classic Le Mans which Win counts as his favourite memory of driving the D-type, despite one slightly worrying moment. 'In one of the races, at night going down the Mulsanne, the car was doing 170mph before the first chicane and I went out around a slower car. What I didn't know was it had just blown up and there was oil all over the road where he was, in the middle to start with and then he'd eased off to the left. And I hit this oil before the braking point and I was on-off the pedal, cadence braking – on-off, on-off, drifting and sliding sideways, lock to lock. I thought, "Oh my God, Nigel, this is going to be a big one." And you know, it stopped literally within inches of the Armco sideways on at the first chicane. I put it into first gear, pulled away and went on again.

'That was scary but otherwise in all four races I did, four sprint races, it was magic, especially in the Porsche Curves where it was fabulous. You look out the side of the car as you're drifting it. Out of all my racing experiences, the "D" is something special. I have wonderful memories, but my feeling is, if you have a "D" don't try and stiffen it and do all the silly things with it. Let the car do the work, let the car drift.'

Andy Wallace

Double winner at 2016 Le Mans Classic driving Nigel Webb's D-type XKD 505

'All my racing experience was with big tyres and lots of downforce. Yes, lots of times at Le Mans, but always with something very, very quick. When I started to drive historic cars the D-type was one of them; and all that you've learnt before, you don't have to throw it away, but you have to turn the whole thing on its head.

'In a modern car it's difficult because everything's happening so fast and you have to be millimetre perfect, razor sharp with your reactions, and if you're not you won't be fast or you'll crash. With something like the "D" it's more difficult to control. You've got tiny little bits of rubber touching the ground – or not, sometimes, as the case may be – you've got very good brakes for the time but, even so, if you want to stop from 170mph going down the straight at Le Mans you've got to think about it in advance, and you really have to get all your ducks in a row to get it stopped and get it round the corner at the right speed.

'I just think it's an honour to drive a car that was so successful in its day, and to be given the chance to try to master driving it. I'm pretty much on top of it now but of all the cars I've been driving, this is the one that's the most difficult to tame. I've driven the Jaguar Mk1, Mk2 and the C-type, which particularly is an absolute pussycat to drive, beautiful handling, everything. And the Mk1 and Mk2 are just a riot to drive. But the D-type is pretty frisky and if you drop your guard it'll bite you, so it takes a little while. The guys working on the car are doing a fantastic job and they've really got it now to a point where I can drive it without worrying – although you always worry when you drive racing cars. But every time I jumped in this one before, I was wary of the fact that it was trying to bite me. Now we've sort of bonded.

'On a modern car you can tailor it around you to your driving style, but with an older car you've got fewer tools at your disposal to do that. You've still got ride heights and springs and shocks and corner weights, those sorts of thing, but nothing in the way of aero you can adjust. I suppose you'd probably say that 30% you can change the car and about 70% you have to change the way you drive it. Which is probably a fair split.

'Even if I go to a circuit I know really well, like Le Mans where I've done thousands and thousands of laps, the first few laps round the circuit in a "D", it's almost like somebody's changed the track; it's different. But after half a dozen laps at Le Mans this year it was fine. This car is so good at Le Mans – it was *designed* for Le Mans.

'It's beautiful looking and it's beautifully prepared. Everything about it is right and if I think back to the guys that used to drive them, they really had to roll their sleeves up and get the job done and they were obviously very good at what they did. It gives you an appreciation of what they did.

'It's a wonderful car. I wouldn't say it was on my list of easy cars to drive, it's definitely near the bottom of that, but it's very rewarding when you get it right and when you can get to grips with it.'

Nick Faure

Raced D-type XKD 502 owned by Paul Michaels of Hexagon in the 1971 JCB Historic Championship

'In my opinion the "D" epitomises the ultimate road/race car. It's so vibrant, and required the true skill of old-fashioned driving, where the power outstrips the tyres, allowing so much control to be obtained through the throttle alone. You sit in the car and just feel that there's a thoroughbred around you ready for the track. You start it up and the hollow roar of the engine coming through the monocoque goes right through your body and sends shivers through you with the expectancy of an enormous thrill. It has a marvellous one-piece feel that allows you complete control through the wheel. The steering is light and extremely responsive, but the combination of all these senses makes it one of the most memorable race cars that I've ever sat in. I've driven many wonderful cars but the "D" has a special place in my heart. Not the quickest by any stretch of the imagination, but the car that pushes all the right buttons for anybody who loves driving in the traditional way with no driver aids, just you and the machine.'

THIS PAGE Nick
Faure drove a D-type
at the Rolex Monterey
Historic Races in 2004.
(Nick Faure collection)

Faure raced Paul Michaels' D-type Jaguar during the 1971 season. 'It was the first of the real historic championships which JCB organised and ran. It was a great thing that Anthony Bamford put on and it was well attended. We had some great drivers, great people – the likes of Neil Corner, Chris Drake and Richard Pilkington – and it was fantastic.

'I had a lot of success with the D-type. I don't remember if we won the class or not but we had enough success so that Paul was happy to carry on the next year. He sold the D-type and ran a Lister and then after that we ran two cars, which were the Lister and the Birdcage Maserati, and I think Gerry Marshall came in and drove the Lister occasionally.

'The "D" was a wonderful car to drift. You could drift it and opposite lock it, dare I say, like a Porsche. It had a very similar sort of feel to it – although it was front-engined, it felt very Porsche-like. The car was, in my view, very responsive to what you wanted to do. You could set it up in the corner to be perfectly balanced very easily.

'I raced one more recently, in 2004 at Monterey, having had a 30-year gap between when I raced Paul's and when I raced this one.

I only had to sit in it, before I'd even started it, to get used to that feel; the memory of what it was like driving it all those years ago. As soon as you turn the key, start it and blip the throttle, you think "Wow!" It was like doing a race the day after I did the last race. It was a different feel to anything else I've ever sat in.'

The passenger's view

'I'll take you for a ride down the lane if you like.' It was an offer I was hardly likely to refuse. John Pearson still uses his own D-type, XKD 543 – which he restored – on the road (see chapter seven) and I immediately jumped at the opportunity for a ride in it. Climbing into the passenger side of a D-type is no easy matter, though. First the metal tonneau cover has to be removed and then you swing one leg into the oval opening and stand on the seat, taking care not to use the surround as a handhold for fear of bending it. Bring the other leg over and then tuck your elbows in and let yourself slide down into the seat, as far as the restricted leg space will allow. Your knees are hunched up in front of you and there's a distinct impression of sitting on the

car, rather than in it. There are no seat belts, or a windscreen come to that. The driver is protected by a wrap-around screen, but the full-width version wasn't introduced until later. This was going to be a real 'pick-the-flies-out-of-your-teeth-afterwards' moment.

Once in, the view is dominated by the long bonnet (even though this is a short-nose version) and the louvres cut into it. On my right is the bonnet-mounted rear-view mirror, and alongside sits John, cocooned behind his screen. Then the engine barks into life and we pull away. Even at low speed the experience is exhilarating. Try to take it in. You're riding in a real 1950s D-type Jaguar. A boyhood dream come true. A few photos, then put the camera down and enjoy it. A short run down the lane and then we approach the village. Heads turn as the glorious sound of the engine heralds our arrival. People smile and you instinctively nod and smile back in acknowledgement. I am in a privileged position.

The ride is a little bumpy yet comfortable, if that makes sense, and I can feel the sense of pride that John still has as he slips easily through the gears. On the way back, with a long, straight lane in front of us, he pushes down harder on the accelerator. The hedgerows become a blur and I feel my cheeks distorting with the sudden rush of air over my face. Or maybe I'm just smiling inanely...

Like all good things in life, it's over all too quickly and I'm soon being helped out. Bucket list: ride in a D-type. Tick. Thanks, John.

ABOVE The view from the passenger seat is dominated by the louvres in the bonnet. *(Author)*

LEFT The inevitable 'selfie'. The D-type's hinged filler cap cover can just be seen over the author's shoulder. *(Author)*

Chapter Five

The owner's view

It might seem like a silly question to ask why anyone would want to own a D-type Jaguar but, nonetheless, three owners past and present explain their passion for the car.

OPPOSITE Andy Wallace lines up on the grid at the 2014 Goodwood Revival in Nigel Webb's D-type, XKD 505. *(LAT)*

119
THE OWNER'S VIEW

Paul Michaels of Hexagon

Ran D-type XKD 502 in the 1971 JCB Historic Championship for Nick Faure

'I'd always wanted a D-type because when I was a kid they were winning everything and it was a part of history. I knew the previous owner and he wanted to sell it, so I thought, that's great, we'll buy it and race it, which we did.'

The D-type in question was XKD 502, registration number MWS 302, which was supplied to Ecurie Ecosse in May 1955 and raced by them throughout that season and the next (see chapter six, 'Individual chassis histories'). At the end of 1956 it was sold to Maurice Charles, who crashed it in 1958 but rebuilt it. By the time it was acquired by Michaels it had been altered quite a bit. Appendix C regulations in 1956 had demanded a full-width screen be fitted and later a luggage compartment was also demanded, but the worst change had been to the suspension.

'Somebody had converted it to independent suspension, and it was hopeless,' explained Michaels. 'When we got the car we went to test it and it was undriveable. So we took it apart, found out what they'd done, and it had no stabilising bars, so in other words the rear axle was steering the car. So we put stabilising bars on it and got it to work. But then, of course, originality became more important and the car was converted back to its original spec, without the silly boot-lid and without the silly screens, and today it's an original car in an original condition.'

Like many owners, Michaels is content to leave the driving to others. 'I drove it at Silverstone once just to see what it was like, but this was before we modified the suspension, and the car was a death trap as far as I was concerned. When we got it working properly we were quite successful racing it. Nick Faure drove it and then I sold it and bought a Birdcage Maserati, which was quite a lot quicker but totally unreliable.'

Michaels admits to regretting selling his D-type and still looks back on it with fondness. 'From our point of view, it was the first car we ever raced and it sent me on to Formula One. We started racing that in 1970 and went from there to the Birdcage, to a Lister, then to a Formula 5000 car and then F1. [Michaels ran John Watson in Hexagon-entered Brabham-Fords during 1973–74.] So in four years we went from a D-type to Formula One. In those days you could do those sort of crazy things. I'm not quite sure you could even dream about it, let alone do it, these days.'

Nigel Webb

Owner of XKD 505, the 1955 Le Mans-winning D-type

Nigel Webb was drawn towards the D-type through his interest in Mike Hawthorn. He has a Hawthorn museum and also owns Hawthorn's rebuilt 1955 Le Mans-winning car.

'It's been a wonderful thing to own, simply, because we've been able to race it at virtually every prominent venue, be it Le Mans or Goodwood or wherever,' he explained. 'We did think of racing it at Monaco, but a long-nose "D" isn't a practical car for there, not having an independent rear end, and Monaco is all corners.'

Although he has driven the car himself, Nigel prefers to rely on professional drivers, such as Win Percy and more recently Andy Wallace, to race his precious possession. 'Once, Win gave it to me at a qualifying venture at Classic Le Mans and I got to about 170mph in it and frightened the life out of myself,' he said. 'Quite frankly, much as the brakes are bloody good on a D-type for what they are, I'm not

an experienced racer, I'm a club racer, I'm not Andy Wallace who races it now. So I know my limitations, let's put it that way, and I keep it that way because it would be criminal to bend it.'

Speaking about his experience of driving the car (see chapter four), Win compared the technique required to master a D-type as being similar to that needed for autocross, where he began competing, and Nigel agrees. 'Because of Win's background – he started on grass, and D-types are all about drifting – he was just incredible with it.'

Nigel has tried driving the car on the road but finds it impractical for ordinary road use. 'Yes, I have driven it on the road and it's a wonderful thing to drive, but it's about as

BELOW Andy Wallace at the wheel of Nigel Webb's D-type, XKD 505, during the Sussex Trophy at the 2015 Goodwood Revival. *(Author)*

ABOVE Win Percy
in Nigel Webb's
D-type at the BRDC
Historic Sports Car
Championship race
at Silverstone in May
2003. (LAT)

practical as a brick,' he said. 'In fact a brick is probably more practical. You can't reverse it very easily, you can't see behind, naturally. We only used it four or five times – the passenger sits much higher than the driver and there's no windscreen on a '55 car. On a '56 and '57 car, of course, there is.'

The reason why the passenger sits so high is two-fold, as Nigel explained. 'One, the toolbox under the passenger seat, and two, the exhaust interferes. Most people don't realise it, but on a long-nose the exhaust runs the total length of the car and on a short-nose it comes out where a C-type does, at the side. And that's not generally realised.'

Nigel is in the fortunate position of owning both a C- and a D-type, and so is in a perfect position to compare the two. 'More people prefer the "D" than the "C",' he said, 'but the "C" is a lovely, practical car. And in my view people prefer the looks of the long-nose "D" to a short-nose. A short-nose "D" is a bit like an ugly duckling, when you compare the two of them. If the long-nose had never been made, then the short-nose would have been fine, but the long-nose is so much more beautiful, it really is.

'They're quite delicate cars,' he continued. 'You cannot abuse them by going over rough terrain and stuff like that. The exhaust on a long-nose is much lower than the short-nose, that's the downside, but bear in mind that old man Lyons [Sir William Lyons] only built the long-nose for Le Mans, which is absolutely flat, so I don't think it ever became an issue. And of course, he never envisaged the long-nose being used as a road car anyway.'

One of the things that Nigel says has always made him smile about the D-type is the very basic instrumentation on them. 'The works cars didn't have a speedometer,' he explained, 'or an ammeter, or a fuel gauge. You've just got oil pressure, water temperature and the tacho – end of story. One of the things that isn't realised is that the rear lights come off a Morris Minor, the voltage regulator comes off a 2.4 and 3.4 Mk1 Jaguar and the early Mk2, which is a small thing of interest. The switching on it is quite special, the light switches and start switch – I think the starter switch came off an aeroplane originally.

'The other interesting thing that Norman Dewis told me, because I asked him once, is why 505 and XKC 004 – which is the C-type I own – hadn't got gearbox numbers. He said, "If it was raced by the factory we didn't put gearbox numbers in, because then the scrutineer could never say it was the wrong number!'"

Stefan Ziegler

Car collector and historic racer

Stefan Ziegler is a big fan of the D-type. 'I like the shape, and I think it's a fantastic race car,' he said. 'You feel really very snug. It wraps around you and feels a very purpose-built car.

'In contrast to the C-type and XK120, with the D-type I very much feel surrounded by the car and part of it, which I really like. You don't get the same feel in an E-type, or lightweight E-type for that matter. You get into the car and you're just part of the car, almost like a Formula One car for me.

'I had always wanted a D-type because I thought it was such a stunning car, so I bought one at one stage, but with no clear plan of what I was going to do. And then, instead of driving it on the road – which is quite difficult in Switzerland – it very quickly came about that I started using it as a race car, which it was meant to be.'

Stefan has owned three D-types in total and feels that the heritage of a car always matters. 'One was a customer car with a bit of racing history,' he explained, 'then I had the most important long-nose D-type for a while, and now I have an Ecurie Ecosse short-nose car which was owned by Dick Skipworth before.'

As to the car's idiosyncrasies, Stefan cites the gear change, with its lock-out pin, the Plessey pump on the brakes and the long tail-fin. 'I think the fin of the long-nose cars is quite unique. It really started a new era in aerodynamics. Not every D-type has or should have the fin, but I think it really makes the car stand out,' he said.

And what about where the D-type sits on the list of the world's most desirable cars? Is it up there at the top somewhere? 'In my view absolutely,' he said. 'I've never driven a GTO or some of the other GT cars, but I always think it's one of the most desirable cars of that era. I would put it on a par with the GTO, the Maserati 450S, maybe the Aston Martin DB4 GT Zagato or DBR1. It's open for debate which is the most important – some are slightly rare, some have slightly more prestige, but I think it's absolutely up there.'

BELOW Stefan Ziegler exits the chicane during the Sussex Trophy race at the 2010 Goodwood Revival. *(LAT)*

Chapter Six

Individual chassis histories

This chapter details briefly the histories of the works and other significant D-types as raced during period. It doesn't claim to be an extensive account, nor to cover the more recent histories of the individual chassis, many of which are still competing in historic racing today.

OPPOSITE Stirling Moss at the wheel of XKD 406, which he shared with Peter Walker, during the 1954 Tourist Trophy at Dundrod. The car was fitted with a 2.5-litre engine for the event in an attempt to beat the handicappers, but a piston failed and the car finished 14th on the road, 18th on handicap. *(LAT)*

Works D-types

The early models of D-type followed the existing XKC chassis-numbering system since, at that time, Jaguar hadn't planned to call the new model the 'D-type'. Six cars were built, XKC 401 to XKC 405 and XKD 406, although 405 was subsequently broken up and used for spare parts to repair damaged cars.

1954
XKC 401

This was the prototype D-type and was never raced, only ever being used for testing and development. It first ran at Lindley on 13 April 1954 and, following further testing at Silverstone, it took part in the Le Mans test on 8 May, setting an unofficial lap record. The car continued to be used for both driver and development testing and in 1955 was fitted with de Dion rear suspension, which was later removed.

BELOW Duncan Hamilton and Tony Rolt finished second at Le Mans in 1954 driving XKC 402. *(LAT)*

XKC 402

Chassis XKC 402 was the first of the works cars to be completed, on 4 May 1954. It first ran at Le Mans in June 1954 with Tony Rolt and Duncan Hamilton taking it to second place. The following month the pair again took the runners-up slot, this time at Reims in the 12-Hour race. The car's only other works outing was at the Tourist Trophy at Dundrod, where the pair failed to finish. After being on display at the Paris Salon, the car was sold to Hamilton in January 1955. He campaigned it throughout 1955–57 with reasonable success, including a brace of wins at Goodwood. Michael Head drove the car to victory at Eläintarhanajo in Sweden in 1955.

XKC 403

XKC 403 also made its debut at Le Mans in 1954, with Stirling Moss and Peter Walker at the wheel. The car retired, but not before it had set a new speed record on the Mulsanne Straight of 172.97mph. The pair also retired

from the Reims 12-Hours that year but managed to finish sixth at the Tourist Trophy. Tony Rolt drove it to third place at Silverstone in May 1955 before it was sold to Jack Broadhead for Bob Berry to drive. In private hands it proved competitive, Berry scoring a number of top six finishes before crashing at the Tourist Trophy at Dundrod in September. It was rebuilt but crashed and rolled at Goodwood in May 1956 (after Berry had scored a victory in it earlier in the day). It was rebuilt again with a new chassis frame and monocoque, the running gear from the original car, along with the engine and gearbox, being transferred over, and Berry scored a victory at Oulton Park later in the year. The following year it was driven by Berry plus a number of other drivers such as Peter Blond, Ron Flockhart, Jack Fairman and Reg Harris.

XKC 404

The third of the works cars at Le Mans in 1954. Driven by Peter Whitehead and Ken Wharton, it retired with gearbox failure. The pair were more successful at Reims, however, taking victory in the 12-Hour race in July, and Jaguar test driver Norman Dewis set FTD at Brighton Speed Trials. Mike Hawthorn used XKC 404 to finish fourth at Silverstone in 1955 and later in the year it was loaned to Duncan Hamilton and Tony Rolt to run in the Goodwood Nine-Hours, the pair retiring. In 1957 it was sold to John Coombs and subsequently to John Love, who ran it successfully in South Africa during 1959–60. It was crashed at the 1961 Kyalami 9-Hours but subsequently restored.

XKC 405

This chassis was never completed and was instead broken up for spares. It is believed that its chassis frame could have been used in the rebuild of either XKC 402 or 403.

XKD 406

This was the last of the 1954 works cars to be built and was designated 'XKD' as opposed to 'XKC', as its predecessors had been. It made its debut at the RAC Tourist Trophy at Dundrod fitted with a 2.5-litre engine, with Stirling Moss and Peter Walker at the wheel. It suffered piston failure, but was classified 18th on handicap. In 1955 it was loaned to Briggs Cunningham in the USA. During tests at Daytona Beach, Phil Walters achieved 164mph. He and Mike Hawthorn then took victory at the Sebring 12-Hours, after which the car returned to the UK and was sold to Duncan Hamilton. It was raced by drivers such as

ABOVE Jacques
Swaters and Johnnie
Claes finished third
at Le Mans in 1955
driving the Ecurie
Francorchamps-
entered XKD 503.
(LAT)

Peter Whitehead, George Abecassis and Michael Head, who finished sixth in it at the Swedish GP at Kristianstad. It was sold in 1956–57 and used for hill climbs and sprints.

1955

Five long-nosed, steel-framed D-types were built, XKD 504, 505, 506, 507 and 508.

XKD 501

This was sold direct to the Ecurie Ecosse team in May 1955. Its first event should have been at Silverstone but Jimmy Stewart crashed it during practice. It was rebuilt by Jaguar but crashed again by Stewart at the Nürburgring. The rest of the year was more successful, however, with Ninian Sanderson and Desmond Titterington at the wheel. Sanderson used it to take sixth at the British Grand Prix meeting at Silverstone and Titterington took a first and a second at Charterhall and won again at Snetterton. He and Sanderson finished second in the Goodwood Nine Hours before Sanderson took a brace of wins at Crimond while Titterington was second at Aintree. Despite being rolled in practice at Snetterton in March 1956 by 'Wilkie' Wilkinson, more success followed, the highlight being victory at Le Mans for Sanderson and Ron Flockhart and other top-three finishes for them and Jock Lawrence during the year. Flockhart drove the car in the 1957 Mille Miglia but retired, and it had a few outings in 1960 before being retired from racing but retained by Ecurie Ecosse backer Major E.G. Thomson.

XKD 502

Also sold direct to Ecurie Ecosse in May 1955. The car's first outing was at Silverstone in May 1955, where it finished sixth driven by Desmond Titterington. This was followed up with victory for Titterington a week later in the Ulster Trophy, but he blotted his copybook by crashing it at the Nürburgring the same month. After being rebuilt by the works, Ninian Sanderson and Bill Smith drove it for the rest of the year, Sanderson taking victory at Aintree in September. The following year it was raced extensively, with Alan Brown joining the driving rota alongside Sanderson, Ron Flockhart, Titterington and Jock Lawrence. Flockhart won at Charterhall, Sanderson at Spa and Titterington at Goodwood. At the end of 1956 it was sold to Maurice Charles who raced it throughout 1957, winning at Goodwood and taking a number of top-three places. It was crashed in 1958 and rebuilt, possibly using the body from XKD 508. Charles continued to run the car sporadically for the next few seasons.

XKD 503

Supplied to Ecurie Francorchamps for Johnnie Claes and Jacques Swaters to drive in the 1955 Le Mans, the pair finishing third. It was sold to Ernie Erickson in the USA and run at the inaugural Road America meeting at Elkhart Lake, finishing third. Erickson took another third at Nassau in December that year and continued to campaign it during 1956, his best result being a win at Lawrenceville. It was sold on again in 1957, this time to Alfonso Gómez-Mena, who ran it in the Grand Prix of Cuba, finishing sixth, and in the Sebring 12-Hours, where he retired. The car's subsequent history is unclear.

XKD 504

This was the first of the long-nosed D-types and was mainly used for testing of the Lucas fuel injection system. It was the spare car at Le Mans in 1955 but was never used. Its first race was at Silverstone in 1956 at the *Daily Express* International Trophy meeting, when Jack Fairman retired with a broken driveshaft. The same year it was raced at the Nürburgring by Paul Frère and Duncan Hamilton after Frère had crashed their race car in practice, but again retired, this time with a broken gearbox. At the end of 1956 it was sold to Ecurie Ecosse and driven to sixth place at Spa by Jock Lawrence. He and Ivor Bueb finished 11th at the Nürburgring before Lawrence took the car to second place in the Forez 2-Hour event at St Etienne. The car was one of three Ecurie Ecosse entries in the 500 Miglia de Monza, otherwise known as the 'Race of Two Worlds' or 'Monzanapolis' event, finishing sixth with Sanderson at the wheel. The car was campaigned again the following year by Ecurie Ecosse but with little success, the best result being at the 1958 Tourist Trophy at Goodwood when Masten Gregory and Innes Ireland brought it home in fifth place. The car then passed into the hands of privateer racer Mike Salmon, who ran it successfully through 1959–61, the high spot being victory in the *Autosport* 3 Hours at Snetterton in 1961. Salmon sold the car to fellow privateer Peter Sutcliffe who ran it in 1962 but crashed badly at Snetterton in March 1963. It was rebuilt using the chassis frame of XKD 505 and later in its life it won the inaugural Griffiths Formula historic race in the hands of Neil Corner.

XKD 505

Works long-nose car driven to victory in its first race at Le Mans 1955 by Mike Hawthorn and Ivor Bueb. This was the year of the terrible accident that claimed the lives of over 80 spectators when the Mercedes of Pierre Levegh plunged into the crowd, resulting in the eventual withdrawal of the rest of the Mercedes

BELOW Mike Hawthorn appears to be giving the photographer a two-fingered salute as he drives XKD 505 during the ill-fated 1955 Le Mans race, followed by the Mercedes 300 SLR of Juan Manuel Fangio and Stirling Moss. *(LAT)*

ABOVE Desmond
Titterington and Mike
Hawthorn drove
XKD 506 at the
1955 Tourist Trophy
at Dundrod, but
retired with a broken
crankshaft. *(LAT)*

team and a slightly hollow victory for Hawthorn
and Bueb. The car was never raced again but
instead used by Jaguar for testing, particularly
of independent rear suspension, until June
1958. After this its history is unknown although
it's thought that it was broken up for spares
by the factory. Certainly its chassis frame was
used in the repair of XKD 504 (see page 129).
In the 1980s this frame was removed from 504
and used to build what is described as 'an
evocation' of XKD 505 using authentic parts.

XKD 506

Another works long-nosed entry for Le Mans
1955, driven by Tony Rolt and Duncan Hamilton
but retired with gearbox problems. In Hawthorn's
hands it then finished fifth at the British Grand
Prix meeting at Aintree but retired from the
Tourist Trophy at Dundrod with Hawthorn and
Titterington at the wheel. In 1956 the car was
loaned to Briggs Cunningham in the USA, with
Sherwood Johnston taking victory first time out
at Walterboro. With him and William Spear at
the wheel it retired from the Sebring 12 Hours
and then continued to be run by Cunningham
throughout 1956–57 before being returned to
the Jaguar works, where it was scrapped.

XKD 507

Entered by Briggs Cunningham for the 1955
Le Mans, where it retired with a broken piston.
Shipped to the USA and driven at the inaugural

Road America meeting by Sherwood Johnston,
finishing second. Johnston then took victories
at Watkins Glen and Hagerstown, clinching
the 1955 SCCA National Championship for
class C modified sports cars, and another
win in Nassau. The car continued to be run
by Cunningham during 1956–58 before being
placed on display in his private museum.

XKD 508

The third works long-nose entry at Le Mans
1955, driven by Bob Beauman and Norman
Dewis until it ended up in the sand bank at
Arnage. Afterwards sent to Briggs Cunningham
and retired from 1956 Sebring 12 Hours with
Duncan Hamilton and Ivor Bueb driving. During
1957 is was campaigned by Walt Hansgen in the
SCCA Championship, taking five victories before
returning to the works and being scrapped.

1956

Six long-nose works cars built – XKD 601, 602,
603, 604, 605 and 606.

XKD 601

Works car, first raced at 1956 Sebring 12 Hours
driven by Mike Hawthorn and Desmond
Titterington. Fitted with Lucas fuel injection
and led the race until brake problems caused
it to retire. It also retired with the same driver
combination at the Nürburgring 1,000km but
finished second at the Reims 12-Hours with

LEFT A pit stop for XKD 601, driven by Duncan Hamilton and Masten Gregory at Le Mans in 1957, the pair finishing sixth. (LAT)

Hawthorn and Paul Frère at the wheel. It was then sold to Duncan Hamilton who raced it throughout the rest of 1956 and 1957–58 before selling it to privateer Peter Sargent.

XKD 602

Works entry at 1956 Le Mans, driven by Jack Fairman and Ken Wharton but involved in an accident early in the race when Fairman spun trying to avoid the already-spun XKD 603 of Paul Frère and was then hit by a Ferrari, all three cars being eliminated. XKD 602 was subsequently dismantled and parts used to rebuild XKD 603 – see below.

XKD 603

Another long-nose works car, it had its first race at the 1956 Daily Express International

BELOW Mike Hawthorn set a new sports car lap record driving XKD 603 at the *Daily Express* International Trophy meeting at Silverstone in May 1956 before retiring with steering problems. (LAT)

Trophy meeting at Silverstone, driven by Mike Hawthorn, but retired. It finished third at the Reims 12 Hours with Desmond Titterington and Jack Fairman at the wheel but was crashed at Le Mans by Paul Frère, who was paired with Titterington. The chassis frame from 603 was then fitted to XKD 602 by the factory to create another 603. At the start of 1957 the car was sold to Ecurie Ecosse and had its first outing at the Buenos Aires 1,000km, finishing fourth driven by Roberto Mieres and Ninian Sanderson. It ran at Spa and the Nürburgring (tenth for Sanderson and eighth for Ron Flockhart and Jack Fairman) before Flockhart took it to victory at the Forez 2-Hours. In June, with Jock Lawrence and Sanderson at the wheel, it took the runner-up spot in Ecurie Ecosse's famous 1-2 at Le Mans. It continued to be run by the Ecosse team for the rest of 1957, including finishing fourth at the 'Monzanapolis' event, and throughout 1958–59 but without any notable success before being sold to James Munro in the USA.

XKD 604

Works long-nose car built with de Dion independent rear suspension as opposed to the usual Salisbury solid rear end. Like XKD 603, its first race was the 1956 *Daily Express* International Trophy meeting at Silverstone, driven by Desmond Titterington, but it was eliminated in a first lap, multi-car accident. It is believed the car was stripped at the works for spares, although one report suggests it went to Ecurie Ecosse.

XKD 605

The penultimate D-type built and fitted with a fuel injection engine, the car won on its debut at the 1956 Reims 12 Hours in the hands of Ivor Bueb and Duncan Hamilton. Its next outing was Le Mans where it finished sixth, driven by Mike Hawthorn and Ivor Bueb, hampered by a misfire caused by a cracked fuel injection pipe. When Jaguar withdrew from racing in October 1956 the car was lent to the Briggs Cunningham/Momo team and entered for the Sebring 12 Hours, where Hawthorn and Bueb finished third. Walt Hansgen then took victory at Lime Rock and the car remained in the States until 1961.

XKD 606

The last long-nose D-type, this car was to have been raced at Le Mans in 1956 by Paul Frère and Desmond Titterington but was crashed in practice and replaced by XKD 603 (see left). In 1957 it was run by Ecurie Ecosse and took victory at Le Mans driven by Ivor Bueb and Ron Flockhart, leading home teammates Jock Lawrence and Ninian Sanderson in the rebuilt XKD 603. It continued to be run by the Ecosse team throughout 1957–58, finishing fifth in the 1957 'Monzanapolis' event driven by Lawrence, while Ron Flockhart took victory at Charterhall in '58. It appears not to have been raced during 1959, but in 1960 – still run by Ecurie Ecosse – Flockhart finished sixth at Silverstone and, paired with Bruce Halford, retired at Le Mans. In 1961 the car was sold to privateer Jack Wober.

Other significant chassis

XKD 509

First production line car, supplied to Homburg, USA.

XKD 513

Sold to Jean-Marie Brussin, who raced under the pseudonym 'Mary'. Finished third at 1957 Le Mans with Jean Lucas. The following year Brussin crashed in the car at the same circuit and was killed.

XKD 517

Owned from 1956 onwards by the Murkett Brothers and raced by Henry Taylor. In 1958 sold to Jock McBain and raced by Jim Clark, entered by Border Reivers. Scored 12 victories.

XKD 518

Raced by Peter Blond in 1956. Subsequently owned by Monty Mostyn of Speedwell Garage, Jean Bloxham and John Coombs.

XKD 520

Raced by 'Bib' Stillwell in Australia.

XKD 573

Ecurie Francorchamps team car.

ABOVE Jean Lucas and Jean-Marie Brussin, who raced as 'Mary', finished third at Le Mans in 1957 in XKD 513. *(LAT)*

LEFT Paul Frère and Freddy Rousselle drove the Ecurie Francorchamps XKD 573 to fourth at Le Mans in 1957. *(LAT)*

Chapter Seven

Restoration and historic racing

The proper restoration of an historic racing car like the D-type is hugely time-consuming and has to be done with meticulous attention to detail. Sourcing components and proving the car's heritage are just part of the process. But when complete, there are plenty of suitable events at which to take it racing.

OPPOSITE The Lavant Cup race at the 2014 Goodwood Revival was held purely for D-type and XKSS Jaguars to mark the car's 60th anniversary. *(Author)*

135

Restoration

The degree of restoration required on a D-type depends, very obviously, on the condition of the car in question, as the story of chassis number XKD 524 illustrates.

The car was exported to the USA and bought by Paul Pfohl, who was best known as a motorcycle racer. The car was one of only four D-types to have been painted black by the factory. Pfohl raced it at various places including Riverside and Watkins Glen and also competed in several hill climbs. The car was used very little until 1967 when it was taken off the road and stored in a barn for over 35 years, only being moved to a storage facility because of the threat of a forest fire in the area. It was then sold by Pfohl's son Bill to a collector from Europe and sent to Pearsons Engineering for restoration.

'We had a D-type in which hadn't run since the mid-'60s,' explained Gary Pearson. 'The guy who originally owned it bought it from a Jaguar dealer in New York. He went down to California, drove around the roads in it, blew the engine up sometime in the early '60s, put it in a barn, and that was it.

'Years later the car turned up. He and his family had moved from California to Oregon and put it in another shed. Then the father and son decided to sell it. This car had been unheard of for years and one of our customers went to have a look at it, met the old guy that bought the car in the first place and his son, and the car was absolutely original. Original paint, everything. The only work that had ever been done to the car was that it had the clutch changed at the Jaguar dealer in New York, and when they put the engine and gearbox back in, they put the gear lever the wrong way round. Other than that, the car was absolutely original. It had got a little dent in the front from when the son was a kid and lent his pushbike against it or something.

'We did a total restoration on it but with as little cosmetic work as possible. Where we had to replace things like the aluminium radiator and the aluminium oil cooler, which had furred up inside, we had to blend these things in. Otherwise it's absolutely original. We had to do a little paint repair on the front of it, an invisible repair, and just T-Cut the rest of the paint up.

'We took the thing to pieces – every last nut, bolt and washer – and it was a bit extreme what we did in this particular case, because it was probably the only completely original D-type in the world. It was as it left the factory, except for the clutch. So every single nut, bolt and washer was taken, cleaned, and oiled. Everything was crack-tested and went back in it. When we got the car down as a bare tub there were grommet holes that had cables and things going through. It took one of our guys three days with one of those bendy tools just emptying the monocoque and the scuttle panel, which is a U-channel with a lid on top, so it's sealed, because mice had been nesting in there for 40 years and it was just full of crap and mouse skeletons and things like that. In the end, the only way to get to it was through a small hole.

'Everything rubber on it was obviously knackered but the thing was beautifully preserved. The leather on the driver's seat had faded, but the colour of the leather on the passenger side, because it was under the tonneau cover with no light on it, was beautifully preserved.

'With most of the cars that we restore, you don't know how many miles they've done or what sort of wear and tear they've had, so the only way you can do them is to take them to pieces and crack-test the critical components – the suspension, steering, pedals, all that sort of stuff, all the safety stuff and replace anything that is cracked. It's probably more dangerous if you have a component failure on the road than on the racetrack, because at least on a racetrack you've got gravel traps and you're all travelling in the same direction. And with something like the Mille Miglia you've probably got more chance of something happening there than you do on a circuit. So we apply the same standards regardless, whether it's a car that's going to be used for the road or going to a collection or going to Le Mans: strip and crack-test everything. Safety and security is number one.'

Restoration of XKD 543

The story of chassis XKD 543 is an interesting one. It was a victim of the fire that swept through Jaguar's Browns Lane premises in February 1957. Unlike others which were deemed to be beyond economic repair and had to be scrapped, XKD 543 was one of the least burnt and was consequently dismantled for spares, the engine being rebuilt and sold to John Tojeiro of the Tojeiro Car Company.

Other items, such as the chassis frame, were eventually sent for scrap, but instead of being destroyed were retained by a scrap dealer in Birmingham. This chassis, together with a number of other parts, was bought in the 1960s by racing driver Gerry Ashmore, with the intention of rebuilding the car.

Ashmore kept the parts for some 40 years before selling them to Jaguar specialist John Pearson. 'Gerry had been a friend for many years, since the 1950s,' explained John. 'He was a very successful driver. The family were Jaguar agents, I think, under a main distributor in Birmingham, and always dealt in sports cars

and suchlike. He bought all this stuff and was going to rebuild it. This was years and years ago and I've had a thing about it ever since.'

Ashmore never did get round to rebuilding the car and, after many years of gentle persuasion, agreed to sell the parts to John, who took respected Jaguar expert and author Paul Skilleter to Saint-Malo in France, where Ashmore was now living, with him to examine the parts and help establish them as being genuine. 'Paul is a great friend of mine,' explained Pearson, 'and he came with me to Saint-Malo and we did it all in a day. Gerry met us at the port and we caught the next night boat back.

'It was important to have a proper Jaguar expert with me to authenticate it. It was just rubbish, like scrap metal. The frame was very rusty, but it was only surface rust and you could

BELOW The component parts of XKD 543 as collected from France by John Pearson. Then-owner Gerry Ashmore stands alongside.
(Paul Skilleter/John Pearson collection)

read the chassis number. Also, Jaguar always used red oxide paint on the frame, and then put the top coat on, which this had. It had the original axle but the engine and gearbox had been sold off. It took years to get the parts to do it. The body and the monocoque are new, and the tail, but we've now managed to buy an original bonnet. The brakes were all burned but the caliper is cast iron, so it blasted up beautifully, and we crack-tested them. And they're numbered and in the build sheet, so the build sheet for the car will have the number of the brake caliper.'

The first task, in the case of a 'barn find' such as this, is to establish the authenticity of the car and its components, and the case of 543 is a good example of how this is determined. In a report written at the time Skilleter states: 'I was present when John Pearson collected [the car] from its then owner. From every aspect this frame and the number XKD 543 stamped on it appear to be authentic. The number XKD 543 is unchallenged and unduplicated.

'I believe that the position regarding the car's physical identity is clear. A D-type was legally identified by Jaguar Cars through its chassis number. The "chassis" in the case of a D-type is the frame which runs from front to rear, the front portion carries the front suspension and engine, while the rear part of the frame is secured to the rear cross-member/bulkhead which carries the rear suspension. The D-type's construction is unusual in that some of the load is borne by the body which is penetrated by the frame. However, although it is load-bearing, this aluminium centre section is clearly defined as the "body" by Jaguar (see factory build schedule etc). It carries only a body number tag, not the chassis number. An accredited D-type carrying a chassis number cannot be built from it alone, any more than a legitimate XK120 roadster can be built from just the bodywork and no chassis frame. The chassis frame is crucial in identifying a D-type Jaguar.

'Should the frame under discussion be incorporated into a running car to correct D-type specification, then I consider that for the purposes of FIA documentation, the resulting entity should be viewed in the same light as other vehicles with papers, ie physically a

D-type Jaguar. The most direct parallel is XKD 544, also based on an authentic D-type frame with an unduplicated number.

'As for the reconstruction of XKD 543, there is, physically, no difference to the situation which would have existed had the car been involved in a workshop fire just last weekend. No one would question the owner's intentions in rebuilding it with whatever new or remade parts were needed – even to the extent of an entirely new frame and body! It is just that with XKD 543, there has been 44 years in between the fire and the reconstruction.'

Skilleter concluded: 'I would suggest that the car as an entity resurfaced when Gerry Ashmore retrieved the frame thirty odd years ago. In his mind it undoubtedly constituted "a car", albeit one that had been written-off. The frame would appear even to have had a continuous, known history – Jaguar, then the West Midlands scrapyard, then Gerry Ashmore, and now John Pearson. However, it should be noted that XKD 543 (like XKD 544) did not leave Jaguar with a bill of sale as a legal entity and this should always be included in the record.'

Another Jaguar expert, Ole Sommer, made the following comments: 'D-type chassis no 543 was definitely dismantled after the big Jaguar fire and was therefore never supplied or invoiced to anybody as a complete car, so the existence as a complete entity ceased at that time.

'The story of the present discovery of what appears to be the original frame plus sundry loose mechanical D-type components (wheels, rear axle, brake components etc) sounds likely and genuine, a resurrected/recreated 543 could on this basis be officially recognised as the only viable contender for the 543 ancestry all provided that possible official FIA-documents explain this situation very clearly.

'Parallels can be drawn to previously acknowledged resurrections of D-types, which were never invoiced by the factory as a complete car, but are recognised today exactly for what they are: recreations with some reasonably documented link to the original.'

Any car, particularly one used for competition, will have many components replaced over the course of its life. These may simply be due to normal wear and tear, but in many cases can

ABOVE **The frame of XKD 543 is mated to the new monocoque.** *(John Pearson collection)*

be as a result of accident damage. Engines and gearboxes are regularly replaced, as are suspension components and wheels, so a completely original car, as it was when it left the factory, is extremely rare. The example of XKD 543 shows that a car can still be regarded as a genuine D-type, even if it has been rebuilt, provided the parts used are genuine.

But John was still faced with the task of constructing a complete D-type from the pieces he had brought back. 'We laid it all out and I couldn't believe how much more I still needed,' he said. 'We wondered how the hell we were going to do it, but it got done, bit by bit, mostly by a chap called Bruce Rawsthorne who had been with us a long time.

'I suppose the frame was the first thing, because it looked such a mess. In actual fact it was beautiful bright metal when it was gently bead-blasted.' To ensure the chassis number didn't get eradicated during the blasting process, John masked off the small section where the number was stamped. 'It's got a clear lacquer on it now,' he explained, 'so that it

can't rust anymore, but there's the number, and you can't invent stuff like that because the rust is right down in it. The rustiest bit is probably where it may have lain in water, but it all cleaned up beautifully, and then it was a question of looking for the correct paint to get it stoved, and Trimite of Uxbridge were very helpful in identifying that.'

Crack detection of the surviving parts was done at a facility near Coventry Airport, but the monocoque and body obviously had to be built from new. 'It was done by a chap called Jim Gibson, who had been apprenticed at RS Panels,' John explained, 'so you couldn't have had a better start working on these sort of things.' Those bits of the suspension that were missing were all replaced with original parts.

Although the engine had been sold on by Jaguar (and despite John knowing its current whereabouts he has been unsuccessful so far in trying to reunite it with his car), finding the gearbox was what he describes as 'a fairy story'. 'A bloke called Alan George, who had started at Jaguar in about 1952

RIGHT The rear
frame in place.
(John Pearson collection)

BELOW Clutch,
brake and accelerator
pedals.
(John Pearson collection)

BOTTOM Brake
calipers show signs
of corrosion but
obviously weren't burnt,
since the aluminium
hadn't melted.
(John Pearson collection)

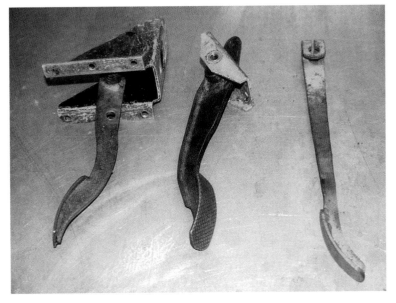

as an apprentice and was probably the best transmission bloke there from the '50s, had bought tons of stuff from Jaguar when he left. He actually had the gearbox with the same numbers on it as were on the build sheet. So he rebuilt it and it's the most lovely gearbox.' The axle, which was with the car, was also rebuilt by Alan. 'That's quite pock-marked,' said John, 'but we didn't have it filled or anything to disguise it.'

Gradually, over time, the car was rebuilt to full D-type specification. It has since been raced a couple of times at Goodwood by John's youngest son, also called John, and at the Le Mans Classic, but today Pearson senior drives it mainly on the road. 'I use it to go shopping at Tesco's,' he said proudly.

LEFT Gary Pearson (left) drives his long-nose D-type at Goodwood, while brother John is in his father's short-nose example, XKD 543.
(John Pearson collection)

BELOW XKD 543 today. John Pearson uses it to go shopping.
(Author)

JAGUAR CARS LTD.

C7263 /tot War...
R 4004?

Date Received 14.1.57   Registration No. Body H.2043   Promised for _____
Car No. XKD 543   Type "D"   Speedometer Reading _____
Colour Black.   Car Bought _____
Name and Address Messrs Jaguar Cars Ltd., Coventry.
Insurance Company _____   'Phone No. _____

1	Engine	Fit new oil filter with all necessary equipment as Schedule A.89, Pages 53 and 54.
2	Gear Box	Remove Gearbox and pass to Gearbox Section for Mod.
3	Clutch	
4	Brakes	
5	Rear Axle	
6	Steering	
7	Springs	
8	Chassis	Change front dampers to C.12334. Change rear dampers to C.12345
9	BODY	Change front anti roll bar to C.12106 Change rear anti roll bar to C.12107 Mod torsion bar levers to C.10519/20
16	Paint	
10	Doors	
11	Wings	
12	Screen	
13	Electrical System	
14	General Items	

DAMAGE AND EQUIPMENT SHORTAGE NOTED ON ARRIVAL | SPECIAL EQUIPMENT
C..1050

W.N.

JAGUAR CARS LTD.

R 40505

Date Received 4.3.57   Registration No. UNREG   Promised for _____
Car No. XKD 543   Type "D"   Speedometer Reading _____
Colour _____   Car Bought _____
Name and Address Messrs Jaguar Cars Ltd., Coventry.
Insurance Company _____   'Phone No. _____

1	Engine	
2	Gear Box	
3	Clutch	
4	Brakes	
5	Rear Axle	
6	Steering	STRIP FOR SALVAGE.
7	Springs	
8	Chassis	
9	BODY	
16	Paint	
10	Doors	
11	Wings	
12	Screen	
13	Electrical System	
14	General Items	

DAMAGE AND EQUIPMENT SHORTAGE NOTED ON ARRIVAL | SPECIAL EQUIPMENT
Change to F.6.

W.N.

LEFT **Worksheet from 14 January 1957.**
(John Pearson collection)

XKD 543 AT THE FACTORY

John Pearson is fortunate enough to have copies of some of the original worksheets covering his car's life just prior to and after the fire at Browns Lane. The first, dated 14 January 1957, a month before the conflagration, shows that XKD 543, which was painted black, was fitted with an oil filter and the gearbox removed for modifications. Changes were also made to the front and rear dampers and anti-roll bars.

A worksheet dated 4 March, only three weeks after the fire, simply states, 'strip for salvage', while another of the same date details the work to be carried out on the engine prior to it being sold to Tojeiro Cars. 'Remove cylinder head and dismantle. Check head for bow. Clean up all valve stems and heads if possible, if not replace if any corrosion or stains. Replenish exterior of head and rocker covers. Repolish inlet ports and remove corrosion from manifold face. Repaint "V". Fit new gaskets, joints "O" rings etc. on re-assembly. Clean up inlet manifold externally and repolish ports to remove corrosion. Fit new adaptor plate and studs.

'Remove sump, check for water entry and/or corrosion in crankcase or bores. Water pump: check for loss of grease from bearings due to heat. If necessary strip pump and renew thrower, studs and bearing assy. Clean up pulley. C/Shaft pulleys etc. Remove clean up to remove all corrosion. Fit new belts, Dynamo and starter. Check for water entry. Clean up commutator, bush gear etc. Fit new Webber [sic] carbs. Fit new manifold.'

Notes written in pencil then confirm the work as it was completed.

LEFT **Worksheet stating that XKD 543 should be stripped for salvage.** *(John Pearson collection)*

OPPOSITE **Worksheet detailing refurbishment of engine prior to it being sold.** *(John Pearson collection)*

UNIT ONLY.

JAGUAR CARS LTD.

Date Received _4. 3. 57._ Registration No. _____ Promised for _____

Car No. _XKD 543_ Type _'D' Type /E 2041.9_ Speedometer Reading _____

Colour _____ Car Bought _____

Name and Address _____ Messrs Jaguar Cars Ltd.,
                            Service Stock.

Insurance Company _____ 'Phone No. _____

1	Engine	Remove cylinder head and dismantle. Check head for bow. Clean up all valve stems and heads if possible, if not replace if any corrosion or stains. Repolish exterior of head and rocker covers. Repolish inlet ports and remove corrosion from manifold face. Repaint 'V' Fit new gaskets, joints 'O' rings etc. on re-assembly. Clean up inlet manifold externally and repolish ports to remove corrosion. Fit new adaptor plate and studs.
2	Gear Box	Remove sump, check for water entry and/or corrosion in crankcase or bores. Water pump: Check for loss of grease from bearings due to heat. If necessary strip pump and renew thrower, studs and bearing assy. Clean up pulley. C/shaft pulleys etc.
3	Clutch	Remove clean up to remove all corrosion. Fit new belts, Dynamo and starter Check for water entry. Clean up commutator, bush gear etc. Fit new Webber carbs. Fit new manifold.
4	Brakes	
5	Rear Axle	
6	Steering	
7	Springs	
8	Chassis	
9	BODY	
16	Paint	
10	Doors	
11	Wings	
12	Screen	
13	Electrical System	
14	General Items	For: The Tojeiro Car Co.,
Barkway, Royston,
Herts.

Handwritten entries (partially legible):

6 — _Glide Head Polished ... Shimmed 'O/D'_
7 — _Cylinder Head Overhauled New Valves ... ..._
8 — _... to be out. Big ends Rebuilt & Reassembled._
9 — _New Piston Rings fitted_
16 — _New Crankshaft Brgs fitted._
    New Weber carbs + in Manifold fitted.
10 — _Bores STD._
11 — _Crankshaft STD. STD._
12 — _Experimental Dept fitted 13-3-57_
13 — _Returned from Expt 15-3-57_

| DAMAGE AND EQUIPMENT
SHORTAGE NOTED ON ARRIVAL	SPECIAL EQUIPMEN
ALL WORK TO BE CHARGED TO F.6	

R. C. Smart.

Neil Corner won the first Griffiths Formula historic sports car race in his D-type, XKD 504, at Castle Combe in May 1966. He is seen here lapping the HRG 1500 of P.E. Martino. *(Neil Corner collection)*

Historic racing

A D-type Jaguar took part in what can legitimately be called the first historic sports car race, when Neil Corner drove his chassis, XKD 504, in the first Griffiths Formula race at Castle Combe in 1966. The event was organised by photographer Guy Griffiths to provide a series in which sports cars of the 1950s could race, and it grew into the Historic Sports Car Club, which today organises numerous events. Corner easily won the event and went on to score many more victories in that inaugural season.

Today the D-type continues to be campaigned enthusiastically by a number of owners, often racing themselves or else employing professional drivers on their behalf. The cars compete around the world at prestigious historic race meetings such as the Philip Island Classic in Australia, the Le Mans Classic, Monterey Classic Car Week at Pebble Beach, California, and the Goodwood Revival.

At the 2014 Revival, the Lavant Cup event was held exclusively for D-type and XKSS Jaguars in order to mark the car's 60th anniversary. Sixteen D-types and two XKSSs lined up on the grid, with the drivers including well-known names such as Nick Mason, Andy Wallace and Derek Bell. The race was won by Gary Pearson in a 1955 long-nosed D-type, from Christian Glasel and Gregor Fiskin.

BELOW Gary Pearson won the Lavant Cup driving his 1955 long-nose D-type at the Goodwood Revival in 2014. *(Author)*